WILLIAM COWPER

by Michael Thorn

GREENWICH EXCHANGE
LONDON

ACKNOWLEDGEMENT

I am very grateful to Dr Ellen Moody, at George Mason University, for taking the time (during one of the American blizzards of 1996) to download and read a version of this text, courtesy of the Internet. Its final form reflects many of the suggestions made in her spirited response.

OTHER BOOKS BY MICHAEL THORN

Pen Friends, Novel

Tennyson, Biography

Alfred, Lord Tennyson - Student Guide

Greenwich Exchange

First published in Great Britain in 1996

Printed and bound by Priory Press, Holywood, N. Ireland.

ISBN 1-871551-25-0

CONTENTS

CHRONOLOGY

1731	15th November (O.S), Cowper born at Berkhamsted
1737	Mother dies
1742	Attends Westminster school
1748	Middle Temple
1750-3	Love affair with cousin, Theadora
1754	Purchases chambers
1756	Break with Theadora Essays published in the *Connoisseur*
1763	Offered high-ranking position Breakdown and suicide attempt Sent to house for insane in St Albans
1765	Leaves St Albans in June Settles in Huntingdon
1767	Rev. Unwin dies in riding accident
1768	Cowper and Mrs Unwin move to Orchard Side, Olney
1770	Brother John dies
1771	With Newton, begins work on *Olney Hymns*
1773	Resurgence of suicidal depression Breaks engagement to Mrs Unwin
1779	Newton leaves Olney
1781	Lady Austen enters Cowper's life
1782	*Poems* published

1783	begins *The Task*
1784	falling out with Lady Austen
1785	*The Task* published
1786	Lady Hesketh visits
1787	suicidal depression
1791	publishes translation of *Homer*
1792	visit to Sussex
1795	Moves to Norfolk
1796	Mrs Unwin dies
1800	Dies 25 April, buried May 2 in Dereham church

WILLIAM COWPER

Introduction

William Cowper was the most popular poet of his period. He remained popular throughout the nineteenth century. If the twentieth century has been less kind to his reputation--there have been various attempts to show that his star has fallen forever, that he was a minor poet who enjoyed an enhanced reputation as many minor poets do--there remains a body of work which is still turned to by the genuine and general reader of poetry. Such readers exist, and their approval is far more important than critical attention in keeping the pilot light of a poet's status alive.

Who does read Cowper nowadays? It is a question asked by those who fail to appreciate him. It sounds succinct, to the point. A question that goes to the heart of the matter. But the answer to it really means nothing. Who reads Pope? Who reads Dryden? I read them rarely. Others are avid admirers. Who reads Shenstone? Who reads Collins? Not many, I suspect. Yet both wrote poems (Collins more) which have lasted. In the end, it is the number and quality of poems which are worth turning back to age after age that must be the measure of a poet's standing. Not the number of takers. Cowper's body of work is larger, more varied, and more accessible than many suppose. It is the work of a major writer.

That Cowper has lost the mass readership nurtured by his evangelical reputation is impossible to deny. But he has never slipped from notice. Indeed, he (rather than his work) has become the focus of notice. His madness, his bizarre reclusive life and odd relationship with Mrs. Unwin have become the things we know about Cowper. We do not know what makes him a great poet. We only know that (as in the pastel portrait by George Romney) he wore strange hats, kept pet hares, and liked his greenhouse. We think he might have been hermaphrodite, or at least mildly genitally deformed. We know that he was barmy.

Any short introduction to Cowper is bound to do the following: consider his madness, and decide how it relates to his art; openly confront the question 'Was Cowper hermaphrodite?'; give an outline of his life, emphasising his relationship with the four important women in it: Theadora, Lady Austen, Harriot Hesketh and, of course, Mrs. Unwin; and, most emphatically, provide a brief commentary on Cowper's poetry and letters.

A Poet who publishes (writing is a different matter) nothing of importance until he is fifty years old and who led, from the age of thirty, a life of apparent idleness and lack of incident, must be approached differently from the artist who enters the fray young and remains active in the world. It is easier to treat that person's life as a piece, or at least a continuous unfolding saga of events, than it is to do the same for a recluse. And yet it is the recluse, the leader of a quiet outward life, whose inner life is the more likely to be one of turmoil. Witness, in Cowper's case, his spiritual autobiography, *Adelphi*, full with visions and voices.

Cowper's inner turmoil was founded in a sense of personal degradation and damnation--a spiritual outcast, he cast himself out of the affairs of his contemporaries, particularly those of his own sex, and sought to lead a quiet domestic life in a small, insignificant English town. In that town there was gossiping to the effect that the relationship between himself and Mrs. Unwin was more than it was made out to be. Cowper, in other words, struck the local townspeople as man enough to be conducting an illicit affair, and too often biographers have been quick to take their cue from Cowper himself and depict him as a 'stricken deer' or, as in the case of his most substantial biographer, by over-emphasising the psychological impact of the death of his mother, to present him as emotionally enfeebled. There are several things wrong with this approach. Firstly, it goes against the grain of what we know about Cowper (who chose his mode of living just as surely as Thoreau elected to live by Walden pond), but more importantly it has been mirrored in an image of the poetry which those more familiar with the life than the work take to have been feeble also--and, when fleetingly strong, as in acknowledged classics like 'The Castaway', strong in a feeble kind of way.

1 LIFE-NOTES (I)

Cowper was born on 26th (O.S. 15th) November, 1731, at Berkhamsted, where his father was rector. Both his parents had high-born blood. His father came from a line of wealthy Sussex land-owners and, through his mother, it was claimed that Cowper was remotely related to the poet, John Donne, and, even more remotely, to Henry III. At the very least, his ancestry was worth several sets of silver tableware.

Some other babies died at birth or soon after but, when Cowper was six, he gained a hale and hearty younger brother, John. In doing so he lost a mother, for she died as a result of the labour. This was, of course, a shattering loss for a six-year-old. But why should it have been so especially shattering, with such long-lasting repercussions for Cowper, at a time when women were all too likely to die in childbirth, and all too many children spent much of their childhood motherless? It is easy, from our own perspective of improved maternity care and psychological knowledge of maternal deprivation, to burden the six-year-old Cowper's loss with too much significance. It did matter to Cowper. It was a hellish thing to have happened. But it did not set him apart; it was not an event to give him cause to feel especially chosen for punishment.

He was sent away to school at Markyate Street, near St. Alban's, where, for two years, according to his own account, he was cruelly bullied. After treatment for an eye condition he went to Westminster, and began to lead a life of happy camaraderie, playing cricket and football, becoming head of his house, and making friends with characters who would grow up to be rakes and true eighteenth-century-men-of-the-world. His closest friend was (Sir) William Russell, whose drowning in 1757 inspired one of Cowper's finest short poems, 'Doom'd as I am in solitude to waste . . .' Although Cowper did not retain these contacts far into manhood, the nature of them is a measure of his ability to establish 'normal adolescent relationships with his peers', as our own bureaucratic educators would put it.

He left Westminster in 1748 and entered the Middle Temple, articled to a Mr. Chapman, a solicitor. During his three years in articles Cowper spent much of his time in Southampton Row, at the home of his uncle Ashley. He and a friend from Chapman's office (the friend was Thornton) visited Southampton Row almost daily and at weekends stayed "from morning to night, giggling and making giggle." The giggling was done with Cowper's cousins, Harriot and Theadora. Through this giggling a love affair developed between Cowper and Theadora, and she was the inspiration for the greater part of his early work as a poet. The Delia poems chart an affair punctuated by trivial lovers' tiffs made over-wrought by the poet's egocentric, self-dramatisation. At this stage in his life, obsession with self was no more than a young man's method of encountering the world. But, in Cowper's case, it did not make him brave. Heightened self-awareness, and a self-consciousness born of a genuinely romantic love which was thwarted by parental objections to his own lack of worldly assets (Cowper was lazy at the law, and showed no ambition) combined to make him nervously insecure.

When he moved from the Middle to the Inner Temple, establishing his own chambers there, despite an outwardly healthy social life (he belonged to the Nonsense Club and, it was claimed, was "able to drink 4 or 5 bottles of claret without sensible effect"), his sense of anxiety increased. Half a dozen years passed before the fateful 1763 arrived. His father had died in 1756. Cowper had become "in a manner complete master" of himself, as he put it in *Adelphi*--man-about-town, bon vivant, contributor of urbane essays to the *Connoisseur*--and much of his later life can be seen as the outcome of a struggle to retain this self-mastery.

The law continued to give him little pleasure. He was not temperamentally cut out for its practice. An opportunity arose, in the early summer of 1763, for Cowper's uncle to offer his nephew a lucrative position as Clerk of the Committees in the House of Lords, and thereby an opportunity of re-establishing the affair with Theadora. Cowper was unable to cope. The emotional demands of the situation were too great. By the end of the year he was in a madhouse, having been subject to psychotic visions, and having made various ineffectual attempts to kill himself. (Cowper used the term 'self-murder', rather than suicide.) He tried to hang himself with a garter suspended from the top of a door, but it fell off. He tried to push a penknife through his ribs and into his heart, but the blade snapped. He tried to poison himself with an opium draught, but at each attempt a physical paralysis prevented him. He took a carriage to Tower Bridge, with the intention of jumping off it, but found the tide at low water.

The trigger for his nervous collapse had been a call to the Bar of the House to defend his claim to the proposed appointment. The prospect of public interrogation terrified him. But the most damaging sense of despair was created in August when, at Margate, he met Ashley and Theadora and, in the words of his biographer James King, "irrevocably rejected her."

Theadora was now an ailing young woman who, the year previously, had been seriously ill with erysipelas. The "psychic process" involved in Cowper's rejection of marriage and a settled career may well have involved the reluctance "to move into the world of experience" which James King speaks of, but why was it dramatised so suddenly, so violently and so dementedly--in a derangement which changed Cowper's life forever?

When he was in the grip of a Calvinistic sense of damnation, Cowper would speak of a "Flaming sword" barring him from Paradise, but at other times he implied a physical abnormality which ruled him out of a normal, marital relationship. The evidence, such as it is, concerning Cowper's alleged hermaphroditism is as follows. In 1834 Southey, who was preparing his biography of the poet, obtained some letters (written by Newton and previously seen by Charles Greville) which stated that Cowper was hermaphrodite, and that this was one of the causes of his morbid state of mind. Greville made reference to the information in his diary, an unexpurgated edition of which was published in 1927. Southey, on the other hand, seeking advice from, amongst others, Wordsworth, decided to suppress the evidence, convincing himself over a period of some eighteen months that the condition was a fantasy, a symptom and not a cause of Cowper's madness. Whatever the truth of the matter, it is clearly demonstrated in Southey's correspondence about this issue that both Newton and Mrs. Unwin appeared to believe Cowper's protestations of physical malformation. A deciding factor in Southey's mind was Cowper's attendance at boarding school. "If the fact had been as he supposed, it was not merely unlikely, but absolutely impossible that he should ever have been sent to a public school," he concluded in 1835.

Absolutely impossible? In fact, it is far more likely that communal living will 'find out' the condition of the 'intersexed' (as the preferred term is today) in the case of those assigned to the feminine gender at birth. A good example is the case of Herculine Barbin, as presented by Foucault. In those designated male, on the other hand, the likelihood is that their male machinery will sufficiently cover other androgynous features. There is no single set of manifestations in the state of androgyny. If Cowper was indeed intersexed, there is no way of being certain how this manifested itself. The penis may have been prevented from obtaining an effectual erection by a membrane on its underside. The head of the penis may have been blind, and the urethral opening elsewhere (though this indeed would have presented problems in the boarding-school urinal). The scrotum may have been malformed, with the testicles only partially descended. There may have been a form of vaginal opening behind the scrotum, or between the two embedded testicles. During adolescence and young manhood males are acutely self-aware of their genital appearance, and even a minor discrepancy from the normal might have led Cowper to believe that he was insufficiently masculine.

However, Southey's explanation is plausible. It is the one which has been taken up by the majority of biographers since. The fact that a piece of genital anatomy is known as 'Cowper's gland' may well have been the starting-point for such a fantasy. Another explanation could be that Cowper fabricated the story in order that Mrs. Unwin was under no illusion that their relationship could be anything other than platonic. If so, it would not be the only time that Cowper made opportune mileage out of his derangement.

Cowper arrived at the Collegium Insaniorum, run by Dr. Nathaniel Cotton, on December 7th, 1763. And did not leave St. Albans until June 17th, 1765--a stay of more than eighteen months. Cotton, who had been trained under Boerhaave in Leyden, and was one of the more progressive doctors of mental illness in his day, ran a small establishment, housing only some half a dozen patients at any one time. Cowper's stay was not, in itself, traumatic, as it might have been in any of the mass asylums of the time. However, when he was eventually well enough to leave, all hope of returning to his previous life, or indeed to London, had been abandoned. It was left to his brother John, now an academic at Cambridge University, to arrange a suitable residence for William. Rooms were found for him in the town of Huntingdon--close enough for John to keep vigil, but not so close as to present a danger of his younger brother intruding too frequently upon his university life.

Cowper was not alone when he arrived in Huntingdon. Accompanying him were two individuals who remained with him, unobtrusively, for many years. One was a servant of Cotton's, Sam Roberts, who had, through attending Cowper, become affectionately attached to his new master; the other, curiously, was a boy of about 7 or 8 years old. Dick Coleman, the story goes, had been rescued from a life of destitute misery in St. Albans. Cowper offered him a new start, becoming his unofficial guardian. There is something faintly suspect about this matter, albeit that most biographers record the detail without comment. The eighteenth century was no doubt more healthy in its willingness to accept an act of altruism at face value, or possibly to take for granted a concealed motive which we might find repellent. We have been educated to mistrust relationships between adults and children whenever they are non-parental, but there is no evidence that Cowper mistreated the boy, either physically or emotionally. That notwithstanding it is strange, and strikes an odd note, to hear of an urchin from the streets being delivered into the care of a mental patient. Coleman must have become acquainted with Cowper while the latter was still receiving treatment from Cotton. The doctor, and presumably William's brother John, must therefore have approved the plan to take the boy away from St. Albans, and thereby remove him from the care of his own father, an alcoholic cobbler. Cowper was frank enough to declare a mercenary interest, viewing his new charge as a potential apprentice valet. The boy would, in a year or two, he suggested to a correspondent, "be old enough to do all the Business for which I shall want him."

Cowper retained contact with only one of his London friends, and that only by letter. Joseph Hill (who had also been to Westminster, was a member of the Nonsense Club and would in due course become secretary to Thurlow) found himself acting as Cowper's financial agent. It was Hill who advised Cowper that he could not remain in the rooms found for him by his brother. It was not that they were too expensive, so much as Cowper was totally uneducated in the matter of keeping house. He wrote to Joe less than a month into his independent existence:

> Whatever you may think of the matter, it is no such easy thing to keep house for two people. A man cannot always live upon sheeps' heads, and liver and lights, like the lions in the Tower; and a joint of meat, in so small a family, is

> an endless encumbrance. My butcher's bill for last week amounted to four shillings and tenpence. I set off with a leg of lamb, and was forced to give part of it away to a washerwoman. Then I made an experiment upon a sheep's heart, and that was too little. Next I put three pounds of beef into a pie, and this had like to have been too much, for it lasted three days, though my landlord was admitted to share in it. Then as to small-beer, I am puzzled to pieces about it. I have bought as much for a shilling as will serve us at least a month, and it is grown sour already. In short, I never knew how to pity poor housekeepers before; but now I cease to wonder at that politic cast which their occupation usually gives to their countenance, for it is really a matter full of perplexity.

The upshot of this mismanagement was that in his first three months in Huntingdon he had spent what should have lasted a full year.

The solution had far-reaching consequences for Cowper's life. On November 11th, 1765, he, and his retinue of two, moved as lodgers into the parsonage of the Rev. Unwin, having, following attendance at church, become a walking and speaking acquaintance of the Unwin son, William. The arrangement was not simply a fortuitous solution to his financial circumstances, but in some part also the realisation of a strangely ardent fixation with finding a place in the Unwin household. He had written to Joseph Hill: "From the moment this thought struck me such a tumult of anxious thoughts seized me that for two or three days I could not draw my mind to any other subject." He found himself praying to God, "Give me this blessing or I die," and when his prayer was answered he viewed it as a response from on high.

Mary Unwin was some half-a-dozen years older than Cowper. Her husband, Morley Unwin, whom she had married when she was eighteen, was considerably older--in his sixties. Mrs. Unwin, who had been known in the town for her cultivated tastes, wide reading and witty conversation, altered the tenor of her life as soon as Cowper moved in, the two of them leading lives of joint evangelical devotion. Cowper, writing to his cousin on October 20th, 1766, gave an outline of their routine:

> Cards and dancing are the professed business of almost all the gentle inhabitants of Huntingdon. We refuse to take part in them, or to be accessories to this way of murthering our time, and by so doing have acquired the name of Methodists... We breakfast commonly between 8 and 9; till 11, we read either the Scripture, or the sermons of some faithful preacher of those holy mysteries; at 11 we attend Divine Service, which is performed here twice a day; and from 12 to 3 we separate an amuse ourselves as we please. During that interval, I either read, in my own apartment, or walk, or ride, or work in the garden. We seldom sit an hour after dinner, but if the weather permits adjourn to the garden, where with Mrs. Unwin and her son, I have generally the pleasure of religious conversation till teatime. If it rains, or is too windy for walking, we either converse within doors, or sing some hymns of Martin's collection, and by the help of Mrs. Unwin's harpsichord, make up a tolerable concert, in which our hearts, I hope, are the best and most musical performers. After tea we sally forth to walk in good earnest. Mrs. Unwin is a good walker and we have generally travelled about four miles before we see home again... At night we read, and converse, as before, till supper, and commonly finish the evening either with hymns, or a sermon, and last of all, the family are called to prayers.

In June 1767, when Cowper had been in Huntingdon for two years, Morley Unwin was thrown from his horse and killed. There was already gossip enough in the town--"black and shocking Aspersion," Cowper called it--and, anyway, both he and Mrs. Unwin had begun to yearn for a place with a more earnest ministry. The Rev. and Mrs. Unwin, in theological as well as other matters, had not seen eye to eye in recent years.

There is not space here to do justice to John Newton. He was five years older than Cowper and had followed his father into a life on the sea, as a merchant sailor. For many years he was involved in the slave trade, but on a sudden conversion (his "Great Deliverance") during a storm at sea, he decided to live a new life. He returned home, married, in due course left the navy, and became a disciple of George Whitefield, associate of Wesley, and public-speaker inclined to Calvinism. In 1764 Newton himself was ordained, as an evangelical Anglican, and had arrived in the parish of Olney in May 1767, only a month before the death of Morley Unwin. He and Cowper were destined to know one another for some dozen years--until Newton's departure from Olney in 1780.

The friendship has assumed mythical significance in some treatments of Cowper--Newton has been portrayed as a Svengali-figure, whose influence had the result of screwing Cowper further and further into his madness--and like most such mythical literary associations it was, on a day-to-day basis, less important to either man than the long-distance view suggests.

After initially being housed at the Vicarage, Cowper and Mrs. Unwin moved into Orchard Side--their home for the next eighteen years--in February 1768, separated from the Vicarage by only a small orchard. The building (which is still standing and now houses the Cowper Museum) fronts onto a small square, and from its parlour windows Cowper was able to observe the business of the town. But it was the back garden, with its greenhouse and summerhouse, which most concerned him. (The summerhouse is still there, but the greenhouse is long gone, its precise location in the garden become a fascinating conundrum for Cowper-followers.)

Orchard Side was the only house in the town, apart from the Vicarage, to have servants. Cowper, who dressed fastidiously in aristocratic style, was known as The Squire. Newton, by his own confession, was socially in awe of his near-neighbour, and during the first period of their friendship was more inclined to follow than to lead.

Cowper's brother John died in 1770, after a long illness. Cowper attended him in Cambridge, and cajoled him into a deathbed conversion, recorded at the end of *Adelphi*. Since moving to Olney, Cowper had been kept unfamiliarly busy by Newton--visiting the sick, copying Bible passages, even (remarkably for one so panicked by public-speaking) leading prayers. In 1771 he was given a new mission--the writing of hymns. These engaged him for much of the '70's. Although by far the greater number of the 348 hymns eventually collected as the *Olney Hymns,* were composed by Newton, Cowper did write 68 of them, and they represent the first fruits of a reactivated poetic utterance. He had written practically no verse since being in the asylum.

The work oversensitized him--whether this was Newton's fault, or a simple matter of the creative process, is a matter of opinion--and he had another bout of suicidal depression early in 1773. Newton stands accused because of the specifically religious manifestation of this period of madness. Cowper dreamed that he was damned, and heard the words "Actum est de de, periisti"--You are done for, perished. In addition to Newton's theological influence, and the effort and concentration of composing the hymns, there was a third provocation for Cowper's mental disturbance. Cowper and Mary Unwin were planning to marry. Mrs Unwin's daughter, Susanna, who had been living with them up until then, was preparing to leave the house, and the 'engagement' might have come about simply to dispel, or rather neutralise, local gossip about their relationship. In any event, it was called off and Cowper was removed from Orchard Side, to be placed in the care of the Newtons. The advice of Nathaniel Cotton, in St. Albans, was sought, but Cowper was not well enough to return to Mrs. Unwin's care until late in 1774. His nightmares continued and he became more of a recluse, never again, for instance, attending a church service.

The admirably succinct and thought-provoking memoir by William Benham, in the introduction to the Globe edition of Cowper's work, states the main case against Newton: "The Calvinistic doctrine and religious excitements threw an already trembling mind off balance and aggravated a malady which but for them might probably have been cured." Newton, apparently, had something of a name for "preaching people mad" and did own up to the fact that at a single time in his parish "We have near a dozen in different degrees disordered in their heads."

Newton was posted to another parish in 1779, soon after publication of the *Olney Hymns*. By this time Cowper was beginning to recover, gardening more, and increasing his correspondence. Although he remained rigidly convinced of his own damnation, his spirits noticeably lightened during the 1780's, his most productive decade.

The departure of Newton coincided with an increased frequency of poetic composition. He began to add poems to his letters, for the entertainment of his friends. At Mrs. Unwin's suggestion, he turned to moral satire, and tossed off 'The Progress Of Error' with such apparent ease that a further three such pieces--'Truth', 'Table Talk' and 'Expostulation'--were finished in as many months. The four poems together, Cowper realised, constituted matter worthy of publication and he contacted Newton, who had overseen the anonymous publication of 'Anti-Thelyphthora' (a protest at his cousin Martin Madan's theological defense of polygamy).

The publication process was long-winded, and Cowper continued to work at pace, with the result that four more satires were added to the volume--'Hope', 'Charity', 'Conversation' and 'Retirement'--making a total of eight. These, and some three dozen shorter poems, were published as *Poems by William Cowper of the Inner Temple, Esq.* in 1782, minus the Preface that Newton had prepared for the book. It was a remarkable collection for a man to be publishing in his early fifties. All of its contents had been recently written--not, as collections of those who publish late frequently are, in fact the work of a much younger man. In this book the public were given the Cowper of there and then, the Cowper of the early 1780's.

2 MORAL SATIRES

There has been a tendency to dismiss the Moral Satires with the argument that they were exercises in evangelical propaganda. Essential exercises, for a poet honing up a talent too long neglected, but ones that the modern reader of Cowper can pass over, now that his reputation rests on other than his evangelical credentials. 'Table Talk', a dialogue between two voices, A and B, in which A acts as a prompt for B, is essential reading. Cowper insisted--against Newton's wishes--that this poem be placed first in the collection. He knew that its very contemporary content would attract readers. The lively political references reveal an attitude of mind much more latched onto his wider world than the popular image of Cowper suggests. He was an avid reader of newspapers. He concerned himself with political issues of the day and was, for example, fairly vocal on two of them--one international (the slave-trade), the other local (the plight of the lacemakers of Olney).

'Table Talk' takes in the Gordon Riots, the war against the American colonies, the death of the elder Pitt, and George III's defense of the crown. Vincent Newey, one of the few writers to publish a full-length book about Cowper's poetry (rather than his life) claims that this poem reveals the poet as a "born verse-journalist". Certainly there was something journalistic in the way in which the main contents of this first book were tossed off at speed. Even in these seemingly compact satires it is possible to discern Cowper's tendency to compose as a series of loosely connected digressions. 'Table Talk', by its very conversational nature, makes this more apparent than in the more serious of the satires, but from each of them it is possible to extract the following type of passage--compact in itself, and yet sowing the seeds of the next thought-process.

I pity kings whom worship waits upon
Obsequious, from the cradle to the throne;

Before whose infant eyes the flatterer bows,
And binds a wreath about their baby brows;
Whom education stiffens into state,
And death awakens from that dream too late.
Oh! if servility, with supple knees,
Whose trade it is to smile, to crouch, to please,--
If smooth dissimulation, skilled to grace
A devil's purpose with an angel's face,--
If smiling peeresses with simpering peers,
Encompassing his throne a few short years,--
If the gilt carriage and the pampered steed,
That wants no driving and disdains the lead,--
If guards, mechanically formed in ranks,
Shouldering and standing, as if struck to stone,
While condescending majesty looks on;
If monarchy consists in such base things,
Sighing, I say again, I pity kings!
TABLE TALK ll.121-140

These are the lines of a sturdy and energetic wit, writing with an instinctive fluency. Note the equal interval between the first four 'If''s, and then the longer pause before the fifth. Cowper claimed to read little contemporary poetry at this time in his life, but he had imbibed well the neoclassic style. Contained within the references to contemporary political and social life, there was a sustained criticism of the prevailing poetic mannerism, a legacy of Pope.

Give me the line that ploughs its stately course
Like a proud swan, conquering the stream by force:
That like some cottage beauty strikes the heart,
Quite unindebted to the tricks of art.
TABLE TALK ll.522-526

The mannerism he objected to was not a matter of style only, but also content.

From him who rears a poem lank and long,
To him who strains his all into a song,
Perhaps some bonny Caledonian air,

All birks and braes, though he was never there;
Or having whelped a prologue with great pains,
Feels himself spent, and fumbles for his brains;
A prologue interdashed with many a stroke,
An art contrived to advertise a joke,
So that the jest is clearly to be seen,
Not in the words--but in the gap between;
Manner is all in all, whate'er is writ,
The substitute of genius, sense and wit.
TABLE TALK ll.532-543

Where 'Table Talk' is good, it is good in short sections such as these quoted. As soon as Cowper attempts to develop an argument at length he is inclined to drift alarmingly from one point to the next. In a discussion which begins as an account of the corruption of the poetic art since the days of Eden, passing through the intolerant days of the Protectorate, and ending up commending a stance of "serious mirth", as typified by John Arbuthnot, creator of John Bull, Cowper throws names at the reader--Horace, Cromwell, Addison--in such a way as to make it very difficult to contain the parameters of his argument. However, his associative method of composition, and apparent aversion to preconceived planning, increase the accessibility of his long poems. He was right to put 'Table Talk' at the front of the book, but if anything it is the later satires, those written while he was waiting for the earlier proofs to go to press, which display him at his most typical, if by typical we mean the Cowper of 'The Task'.

'The Progress Of Error'--in fact written before 'Table Talk'--is witheringly critical of the education indulged in by young members of the aristocracy.

We give some Latin, and some Greek,
Teach him to fence and figure twice a week,
And, having done, we think, the best we can,
Praise his proficiency and dub him man.
From school to Cam or Isis, and thence home,
And thence with all convenient speed to Rome,

With reverend tutor clad in habit lay,
To tease for cash, and quarrel with all day;
With memorandum-book for every town,
And every post, and where the chaise broke down
His stock a few French phrases got by heart,
With much to learn but nothing to impart,
The youth, obedient to his sire's commands,
Sets off a wanderer into foreign lands...
THE FORTRESS OF ERROR ll.365-378

'Truth' opens with a series of bitingly satirical portraits of various religious types--the Pharisee; the hermit; the Brahmin; the seventeenth-century church-goer. The picture of Miss Bridget which begins at line 131 ('Yon ancient prude, whose withered features show...) is often quoted, and its resemblance to an engraving by Hogarth commented upon. That Cowper should have based his description on such a print is possible, but doubtful. The picture sizzles with the poet's first-hand knowledge of such ladies, from his church-attending days.

She, half an angel in her own account,
Doubts not hereafter with the saints to mount,
Though not a grace appears on strictest search,
But that she fasts, and, item, goes to church.
Conscious of age, she recollects her youth,
And tells, not always with an eye to truth,
Who spanned her waist, and who, where'er he came,
Scrawled upon glass Miss Bridget's lovely name,
Who stole her slipper, filled it with Tokay,
And drank the little bumper every day.
Of temper as envenomed as an asp,
Censorious, and her every word a wasp;
In faithful memory she records her crimes,
Or real or fictitious, of the times;
Laughs at the reputations she has torn,
And holds them dangling at arm's length in scorn.
Such are the fruits of sanctimonious pride,
Of malice fed while flesh is mortified...
TRUTH ll.149-166

Pride is the sin which undoes each of the illustrative types. The 'truth' of 'bliss' lies in untutored, unsophisticated belief. Voltaire is compared with a cottage-woman at her sewing-wheel:

O happy peasant! O unhappy bard!
His the mere tinsel, hers the rich reward;
He praised perhaps for ages yet to come,
She never heard of half a mile from home:
He lost in errors his vain heart prefers,
She safe in the simplicity of hers.
TRUTH ll. 331-336

This is simplicity simply, but emphatically, praised. The sinners, the damned, are the proud and voluptuous, the cynical, the scheming. The poem is a call to Christian faith, although at the end Cowper acknowledges that some living in other times, in other places, have found other ways to exalt their minds and live in a state of grace.

But let not him that shares a brighter day
Traduce the splendour of a noontide ray,
Prefer the twilight of a darker time,
And deem his base stupidity no crime;
The wretch who slights the bounty of the skies,
And sinks, while favoured with the means to rise,
Shall find them rated at their full amount,
The good he scorned all carried to account.
TRUTH ll.539-546

Cowper said of this poem, "[I wrote it] on purpose to inculcate the eleemosynary character of the Gospel, as a dispensation of Mercy in the most absolute sense of the word, to the exclusion of all claims of Merit on the part of the Receiver. Consequently to set the brand of Invalidity upon the Plea of Works, and to discover upon Scriptural ground the absurdity of that Notion which includes a Solecism in the very term of it, that Man by Repentance and good works may deserve the Mercy of his Maker."

By 'eleemosynary' Cowper meant that the Gospel (and therefore God's mercy) is freely given. It does not have to be deserved. His insistence on the invalidity of good works is straightforward enough, although in this he was not in tune with all his evangelical friends (including Mrs. Unwin's son, William). The inclusion of repentance as another invalid route to God's mercy was more radical. The logic meant that no one could choose their own salvation. That choice was made by God alone. In this sense Cowper was a Calvinist, believing in the elect (and therefore the non-elect). Those left unchosen, like himself, were condemned to be excluded, cast out. His depressive states were deeply influenced by this fatalistic attitude, and if the Calvinist strain stemmed from Newton, he could well be accused of bearing a responsibility for Cowper's most harrowing despondencies. But there is no evidence to show that Cowper was so influenced. Rather, the impression is that Cowper, from the moment he became capable of self-analysis, felt himself to be temperamentally debarred from any kind of happiness, whether it be emotional (with Theadora) or religious (with God). As in the case of most psychotic derangements, Cowper's bouts of madness were unassailable by rational influence or spiritual ministry. The only effectual treatment was isolation and medication, the latter increasingly consisting of very large doses of opium.

Norman Nicholson called the Moral Satires "Calvinist tracts worked into verse that is competent, but, on the whole, not very attractive." And added, "They have an old-maidish bite." The old-maidishness stems in part from the fact that nobody writes sermonising verse of this type nowadays. But at one time these Moral Satires, straightforward homilies in rhyming couplets, just the right length to read in a sitting, either quietly or aloud by the fireside, were the most widely read of all Cowper's works. They informed the religious outlook of several generations of Christians. Volumes were annotated, passages underlined, and the extent to which Cowper's language has entered the mainstream of Christian thought is exemplified in *A Dictionary Of Biblical Tradition In English Literature* (1992), edited by D. L. Jeffrye, which abounds in references to and quotations from Cowper's works, the majority from the satires.

"Why weeps the Muse for England?" begins 'Expostulation', in a thirty-line tribute to a land rich in material comfort. "Her fields a rich expanse of corn." And commerce at hand, "To pour her golden tide through all her gates." Why weep? Because of spiritual error, fed by rhetoric and artifice. Cowper's plainness of style is put to old-maidish purpose in this poem, which accuses the Judaeo-Christian tradition of having lost the way. Not that, according to Cowper, in the hyper-critical mood he is in in this work, the way was ever a particularly golden one. From the early days in Israel there was "Adultery neighing at his neighbour's door;/Oppression labouring hard to grind the poor." (ll.39,40). Even in worship "Hypocrisy, formality in prayer,/And the dull service of the lip, were there." (ll.43,44). The women were idle flirts. "They stretched the neck, and rolled the wanton eye,/And sighed for every fool that fluttered by." (ll.53,54). The capture and destruction of Jerusalem was the direct consequence of such a fall from grace.

For Cowper's contemporary readers, the subtext of his diatribe against the Israelites, and then the Pharisees, was a parallel criticism of the church in his own time. "When nations are to perish for their sins,/'Tis in the church the leprosy begins;" (ll.96,97). Evangelicals and Methodists alike would have said their hear-hear's to Cowper's portrayal of established church congregation behaviour. "As soldiers watch the signal of command,/They learn to bow, to kneel, to sit, to stand;/Happy to fill religion's vacant place/With hollow form, and gesture, and grimace." (ll.119-122).

The lapse from grace of the Israelites is especially to be condemned since "They, and they only, amongst all mankind/Received the transcript of the eternal mind," (ll.197,198) and were blessed, in their early history, with so many divine interventions on their behalf, which Cowper lists in the section ll.161-196. "Ask now of history's authentic page,/And call up evidence from every age;/Display with busy and laborious hand/The blessings of the most indebted land." (ll.161-164). This passage goes on to present the case of the prosecution in a manner which shows that, for all his desultory lack of enthusiasm for the law, Cowper had caught the cadences of legalistic argument. Israel's position as the chosen people is undone, as a result of sins of the father.

Line 270 begins the case against the England of Cowper's own time; and by line 340 he is ready for an onslaught of concerted power, which sees the verse-journalist in him writing to full effect:

Hast thou, though suckled at fair Freedom's breast,
Exported slavery to the conquered East?
Pulled down the tyrants India served with dread,
And raised thyself, a greater, in their stead?
Gone thither armed and hungry, returned full,
Fed from the richest veins of the Mogul,
A despot big with power obtained by wealth,
And that obtained by rapine and by stealth?
With Asiatic vices stored thy mind,
But left their virtues and thine own behind;
And, having trucked thy soul, brought home the fee,
To tempt the poor to sell himself to thee?
EXPOSTULATION ll.364-375

Only by being read aloud does the force of Cowper's case make itself fully apparent; not in the soft voice of an 'old-maid', but the loud stentorian tones of a lawyer echoing round the courtroom. Cowper uses the staccato rhythm of his rhyming couplets to expert effect, often placing sneering emphasis on the rhyming word, and scoring heavy advantage by sometimes sustaining rhymes for insistent effect:

Canst thou dream there is a power
In lighter diet at a later hour,

To charm to sleep the threatenings of the skies,
And hide past folly from all-seeing eyes?
The fast that wins deliverance, and suspends
The stroke that a vindictive God intends,
Is to renounce hypocrisy; to draw
Thy life upon the pattern of the law;
To war with pleasures idolized before;
To vanquish lust, and wear its yoke no more.
All fasting else, whate'er be the pretence,
Is wooing mercy by renewed offence.
EXPOSTULATION ll.402-413

Draw/law/war(internal rhyme)/before/no more -- these five rhymes (not, of course, underscored in the original) are the table-thumping turbodrivers of the passage. Cowper ends his expostulation, or earnest complaint, with an appeal to mercenary self-interest. For its own literal self-defence England must mend its ways and embrace truth, else its "strength would fail, opposed against the push/And feeble onset of a pygmy rush." (ll.706,707).

With its emphasis on the downfall of the people of Israel, 'Expostulation' was in danger of promoting a pessimistic, fatalistic message. 'Hope' also begins solemnly:

Ask what is human life--the sage replies,
With disappointment lowering in his eyes,
A painful passage o'er a restless flood,
A vain pursuit of fugitive false good,
A scene of fancied bliss and heartfelt care,
Closing at last in darkness and despair.
HOPE ll.1-6

Virginia Woolf, before she had read 'The Task', imagined it to be a sort of diluted 'Paradise Lost'. Later, in her essay 'Cowper and Lady Austen', she had come to recognize that Cowper was his own man, capable of an "intensity of vision that gives his poetry, with all its moralising and didacticism, its unforgettable qualities. It is this that makes passages in 'The Task' like clear windows let into the prosaic fabric of rest." But Woolf, a fellow depressive, could also see that the quiet life, put into place for Cowper by kind friends, was ultimately powerless in the face of his underlying despair. "But what if you are damned, if you are solitary, if you are cut off from God and man, what does human kindness avail?" Certainly, in 'Hope', the strongest passages are those which describe its counterpoint: pessimism, despair, a life of sensuous idleness, false philosophy. Cowper identifies himself so vividly with these states, that when the countervailing paeans to Hope appear, as in lines 153-178, they strike the reader as stilted, the repeated word 'Hope' not (this time) carrying a barrister's commitment to his case, but trotted out like a politician on the stump. The imagery used to support it is, unusually for Cowper, wishy-washy - hope "On speeding wing sails through the immense abyss,/Plucks amaranthine joys from the bowers of bliss..." - whereas Cowper's examples of human error are vivid in their actuality. And this poem, potentially the most positive and optimistic in outlook, bears the stamp of Calvinism much more strongly than the other satires.

But Conscience, in some awful silent hour,
When captivating lusts have lost their power,
Perhaps when sickness, or some fearful dream,
Reminds him of religion, hated theme!
Starts from the down, on which she lately slept,
And tells of laws despised, at least not kept:
Shows with a pointing finger, and no noise,
A pale procession of past sinful joys,
All witnesses of blessings foully scorned,
And life abused, and not to be suborned.
"Mark these," she says; "these, summoned from afar,
Begin their march to meet thee at the bar;
There find a Judge inexorably just,
And perish there, as all presumption must."
HOPE ll.215-228

The poem saves its most withering censure for those dissembling Christians who are able blithely to argue away the importance of their sins, in terms both of compensating good works, and God's all-abundant mercy.

Likewise, 'Charity' is very much a product of Whitefield's teaching (via Newton). The issue of good works was central to the Methodist and Evangelical debate, so there were many poems written on the subject. Cowper, like Hannah More in 'Ode To Charity', was keen to define the quality in terms of benevolent actions towards fellow human beings stemming, not from a compassionate sense of social sympathy, but from a belief in God.

This satire also contains an impassioned denunciation of slavery, to which Cowper was implacably opposed. For a long time he contemplated a poem devoted to the subject and, in the eighties, prompted finally by Hannah More's 'Slavery', he composed 'The Negro's Complaint', 'Pity For Poor Africans' and 'The Morning Dream'. The first of these proved almost as popular as 'John Gilpin'. A few years afterwards he was indignant when a rumour went round that he had changed his position on discovering that, before the advent of slave traffic, Africans had been so numerous that they had been forced into cannibalism to keep numbers down. After unabashedly confessing to a continuing use of rum and sugar, in a letter to a Rev. Joseph Jekyll Rye in 1792, Cowper stated: "I think it better the Negroes should even eat one another, than that we should carry them to market."

Cowper's disdain for a faith in good works as a comforting insurance policy (do enough good things to outbalance the bad) certainly did not mean that he failed to admire genuine philanthropic activity. The hero of this poem--the archetype of Charity in action-- is John Howard (1726-1770), prison reformer, who made hazardous journeys throughout Europe highlighting the appalling conditions in penal establishments. His *State Of The Prisons* had been published in 1777.

As has already been noted, Cowper was never at his best when trying to hold and sustain a subject over a long period. Only in its second half does 'Charity' become a poem of true distinction, Cowper loosening his hold on his chosen theme and allowing his focus to shift. If any one thing makes him worth reading still, it is his extraordinary self-knowledge, on which all his observations were founded. In Cowper's reckoning, self-knowledge presupposed an acceptance of the fact that human reason was in constant need of that "rich possession", divine guidance.

This is indeed philosophy; this known,
Makes wisdom, worthy of the name, his own;
And without this, whatever he discuss,--
Whether the space between the stars and us;
Whether he measure Earth, compute the sea,
Weigh sunbeams, carve a fly, or split a flea;
......
Self-knowledge truly learned, of course implies
The rich possession of a nobler prize;
For self to self, and God to man revealed
(Two themes to Nature's eye forever sealed),
Are taught by rays, that fly with equal pace
From the same centre of enlightening grace.
....
The ties of Nature do but feebly bind;
And Commerce partially reclaims mankind;
Philosophy, without his heavenly guide,
May blow up self-conceit, and nourish pride,
But, while his province is the reasoning part,
Has still a veil of midnight on his heart:
CHARITY ll349-354,359-364,371-376

Philosophy indeed and, we might add, metaphysical writing of the highest order. After sliding back into the anecdotal, with a vivid picture of a squire (for selfish, self-serving reasons) dipping his hand into his pocket in order to help the victims of a national disaster ("From motives such as his, though not the best,/Springs in due time supply for the distressed."), Cowper addresses the reader:

But lest I seem to sin against a friend,

And wound the grace I mean to recommend,
(Though vice derided with a just design
Implies no trespass against love divine,)
Once more I would adopt the graver style;
A teacher should be sparing of his style.
CHARITY ll.485-490

and then turns to examining his chosen medium, the satire.

Most satirists are indeed a public scourge;
Their mildest physic is a farrier's purge;
Their acrid temper turns, as soon as stirred,
The milk of their good purpose all to curd.
...
A thousand names are tossed into the crowd;
Some whispered softly, and some twanged aloud;
...
Strange! how the frequent interjected dash
Quickens a market, and helps off the trash;
The important letters that include the rest
Serve as a key to those that are suppressed;
Conjecture gripes the victims in his paw,
The world is charmed, and Scrib escapes the law.
So, when the cold damp shades of night prevail,
Worms may be caught by either head or tail;
Forcible drawn from many a close recess,
They meet with little pity, no redress;
Plunged in the stream, they lodge upon the mud,
Food for the famished rovers of the flood.
CHARITY ll. 501-504,517-518,521-532

The seventh moral satire, 'Conversation', continues, at least in its first half, in this breezy tone. Speaking of his dislike for argument, Cowper paints a picture of himself as compliant and submissive:

Vociferated logic kills me quite,
A noisy man is always in the right;
I twirl my thumbs, fall back into my chair,
Fix on the wainscot a distressful stare,
And when I hope his blunders are all out,

Reply discreetly, "To be sure--no doubt."
CONVERSATION ll113-119

This is highly amusing and well-observed, especially to be appreciated by those similarly disposed to buckle beneath the onslaught of a gauche garrulity. Nevertheless, Cowper knows his own mind, and the poem quickly becomes a litany of his pet hatreds: long-winded story-tellers ("Salutary weavers of long tales/Give me the fidgets, and my patience fails"); pipe smoking ("Thy worst effect is banishing for hours/The sex whose presence civilises ours"); dandies ("I cannot talk with civet in the room/A fine puss-gentleman that's all perfume"); those who take delight in their own ailments ("They thought they must have died, they were so bad;/Their peevish hearers almost wish they had").

Cowper has himself in mind when he accounts for the bashfulness of certain types:

I pity bashful men, who feel the pain
Of fancied scorn and undeserved disdain,
And bear the marks upon a blushing face
Of needless shame, and self-imposed disgrace.
Our sensibilities are so acute,
The fear of being silent makes us mute.
We sometimes think we could a speech produce
Much to the purpose, if our tongues were loose;
But being tied, it dies upon the lip,
Faint as a chicken's note that has the pip:
Our wasted oil unprofitably burns,
Like hidden lamps in old sepulchral urns.
Few Frenchmen of this evil have complained;
It seems as if we Britons were ordained,
By way of wholesome curb upon our pride,
To fear each other, fearing none beside.
The cause perhaps enquiry may descry,
Self-searching with an introverted eye,
Concealed within an unsuspected part,
The vainest corner of our own vain heart:

For ever aiming at the world's esteem,
Our self-importance ruins its own scheme;
In other eyes our talents rarely shown,
Become at length so splendid in our own,
We dare not risk them into public view,
lest they miscarry of what seems their due.
True modesty is a discerning grace,
And only blushes in the proper place;
But counterfeit is blind, and skulks through fear,
Where 'tis a shame to be ashamed to appear:
Humility the parent of the first,
The last by Vanity produced and nursed.
CONVERSATION ll.347-378

Once again this passage demonstrates self-awareness and psychological penetration. Self-knowledge breeds self-disdain. Here it is sanely and soberly articulated, but it is easy to see how "in the vainest corner" of Cowper's "own vain heart", the self-disdain might become manically exaggerated.

James King says of the final moral satire, "It is only in 'Retirement'...that the writer of 'The Task' begins to emerge. This poem, in many ways a rehearsal for the later poem, possesses the greatest strength of all the moral satires because it is only here that Cowper's 'modish dress' is worn with ease and the fear of art put aside." This is partly true, and reflects general opinion, but the earlier satires should not so readily be put in the shade. As I hope the selected quotations have shown, there is much in them to admire. They are highly accessible, occasionally witty, occasionally metaphysical, not very often satirical, and only very rarely the hectoring religious tracts they are sometimes purported to be. Yes, Cowper did loosen up in 'Retirement', in a manner which he carried over into 'The Task'. This was not a question of dramatically and suddenly changing his style; more a case of continuing and strengthening tendencies already evident throughout the burst of work which led to the publication of *Poems*.

Fin de siècle poets, active at the end of a century and between traditionally demarcated literary periods, lend themselves to debate as to whether they were forerunners (in Cowper's case, was he a forerunner of Romanticism?); or harkers-back (as in Donald Davie's classification of Cowper as "a defiant rearguard"); or simply oddities, impossible to pigeon-hole.

On balance, Davie's view in this regard seems the most sensible. Cowper certainly would not have wanted to consider himself a pioneer in any sense. Politically, too, his allegiances were with the old guard--he was a staunch Whig. But of course he influenced the Romantics, especially Wordsworth who, born in 1770, was already a young man during the upsurge of Cowper's fame and fortune. What was new and original in Cowper was his trenchant self-analysis. Verse-journalists and satirists were two-a-penny in those days, and there were a score of them adept at analysing others. Cowper himself could paint witheringly perceptive vignettes of other types and characters. But his principle interest was himself and, by extension, those with a similar disposition to his own. The passage beginning "Ye groves... ..." (line 365), in the middle of 'Retirement'--ostensibly lines spoken by a reminiscing elder statesman--unquestionably gives us a foretaste of the voice in 'The Prelude':

Ye saw me once (ah, those regretted days,
When boyish innocence was all my praise!)
Hour after hour delightfully allot
To studies then familiar, since forgot,
And cultivate a taste for ancient song,
Catching its ardour as I mused along;
Nor seldom, as propitious heaven might send,
What once I valued and could boast, a friend,
Were witnesses how cordially I pressed
His undissembling virtue to my breast;
Receive me now, not uncorrupt as then,
Nor guiltless of corrupting other men,

But versed in arts, that, while they seem to stay
A fallen empire, hasten its decay.
To the fair haven of my native home,
The wreck of what I was, fatigued I come;
RETIREMENT ll.371-386

However, it is not my impression as I read 'Retirement' (I suppose a statistically-minded research student might undertake a mathematical analysis, stating the relative proportions for different satires) that the prevalence of such passages is significantly greater than in Cowper's other long poems of this period. The determination to suggest they are is born of an impulse to demonstrate a smooth and accelerating development from 'The Progress Of Error' through to 'The Task'. But there is a trap here and the bait is the temptation to approach Cowper--a poet only just beginning to write fluently and prolifically at the age of fifty--as if he were a much younger man. Of course, older men change too, and the very act of writing produces changes of itself. But there is really not so much difference between the satires and 'The Task'.

The common perception today can best be summarised as holding that if Cowper is worth reading at all it is for passages in 'The Task', his letters, and a few short lyrics. The satires are dismissed as Newton-influenced religious tracts. This is strange because we can take, almost at random, lines of moralising about card-playing and dancing from one of the satires, and find almost identical ones in 'The Task'. Indeed, that much longer poem is no less a satire than the poems in Cowper's first book. And in both--the mock-epic and the shorter long poems (if it is not too tautologous to describe them thus)--the true satirical subject-matter is awareness of self and of God. However one manages one's life to suit one's personal tastes, the quality and nature of one's mental processes remain all-important. 'Retirement' is no straightforward hymn to retreat and solitude. Its whole purpose, as expressed to Newton, was "to direct to the proper use of the opportunities it affords for the cultivation of man's best interests; to censure the vices and follies which people carry with them into their retreats, where they make no other use of their leisure than to gratify themselves with the indulgence of their favourite activities, and to pay themselves by a life of pleasure for a life of business." The last words of this suggest that Cowper would be aghast to find what the word 'retirement' has come to mean to the average man and woman today.

Of the shorter poems included in Cowper's first volume, 'Verses, Supposed To be Written by Alexander Selkirk During His Solitary Abode On The Island Of Juan Fernandez' is the best-known, beginning, as it does, with the frequently quoted line "I am monarch of all I survey". Selkirk [1676-1721] was a Scottish sailor who, after a quarrel at sea, demanded to be put ashore on an uninhabited island in the Fernandez group, where he languished for four years and four months. Defoe's *Robinson Crusoe* published in 1719, was firmly based on Selkirk's published account of his experiences, which he was fortunate enough to be able to produce after being rescued in 1709.

From its opening line, the simplicity and confidence of Cowper's diction portray a character with the fortitude to withstand "this horrible place". Although the poem speaks of despair, it ends with Selkirk settling down in his cabin, reconciled to his self-chosen lot. It is important that readers of the poem know--as Cowper's contemporary readers would certainly have known, but which a modern student of Cowper will need to be told--that Selkirk's abandonment was voluntary. He asked to be put off his ship. So, when we read the poem, the thought crosses our mind--yes, Cowper had also, in a sense, voluntarily set himself down upon an island. And this poem, together with the others in the volume, constituted his message in a bottle, floated out to his associates in the wider world.

My friends,--do they now and then send
A wish or a thought after me?
O tell me I yet have a friend,
Though a friend I am never to see.

Interestingly, the poem which followed this, in the sequence as originally published, was 'On The Promotion Of Edward Thurlow Esq.', and as Cowper had insisted on having his own way in deciding which satire would open the book, we can imagine that he was no less strong-willed in the matter of the shorter poems' sequence. The contiguity of these two poems is therefore highly significant.

Reviewers praised the shorter poems, at the satires' expense. " 'Table Talk', 'The Progress Of Error', 'Truth', 'Hope' and 'Charity' are laboured pieces of considerable length, but the greatest part of the volume consists of lively sallies, called by the French jeux d'esprit," was the *London Magazine's* inaccurate and inapposite comment. Even the shorter poems (taking up, at most, a quarter of the volume) were hardly jeux d'esprit. The *Critical Review* was of like mind. "Towards the end of the volume are some little pieces of a lighter kind, which, after dragging through Mr. Cowper's long moral lectures, afforded us some relief... It is a pity that our author had not confined himself altogether to this species of poetry, without entering into a system of ethics for which his genius seems but ill adapted." The most favourable notice appeared in the *Monthly Review*, which greeted a new, individual voice: "He is a poet sui generis, for as his notes are peculiar to himself, he classes not with any known species of bards that have preceded him: his style of composition, as well as his modes of thinking, are entirely his own."

By the time these reviews appeared (after publication in March 1782), Cowper had already met Lady Austen, the inspiration of his next book. The first one did not sell, and the friends Cowper sent copies to (Thurlow and Colman in particular) did not acknowledge them. But the American, Benjamin Franklin, ordered a copy.

3 LIFE-NOTES (II)

Cowper was extraordinarily forward in making the acquaintance of Lady Austen. He was watching the square from his window one day, in the summer of 1781, when he saw two sisters out shopping together. Just as earlier he had formed a determination to move in with the Unwins, he was seized by a sudden impulse to be introduced to the more attractive of these two women. He insisted Mrs. Unwin go out into the street and invite them in for tea. A few months later he was to write, in a poem titled 'A Poetical Epistle To Lady Austen':

Mysterious are His ways, whose power
Brings forth that unexpected hour,
When minds that never met before,
Shall meet, unite, and part no more:
It is the allotment of the skies,
The hand of the Supremely Wise,
That guides and governs our affections,
And plans and orders our connexions:
Directs us in our distant road,
And marks the bounds of our abode.
Thus we were settled when you found us,
Not dreaming of so dear a friend,
Deep in the abyss of Silver End.

Lady Austen was in her mid forties when she first walked into the parlour at Orchard Side. After her husband, Robert Austen, whom she had married when she was nineteen, had succeeded to a baronetcy, the couple spent much of their life in Sancerre, France. Lady Austen was converted to the Evangelical cause during the 1760's. Her husband died in 1772 and the widowed and childless Lady Austen attempted, unsuccessfully, to find a house near Olney, where she had family connections. She returned to Sancerre, but finally left France in 1778, when political relations with Britain soured during the American War of Independence. Since then she had resided in London, occasionally paying her sister a visit. Cowper, in hindsight, and reflecting on Lady Austen's period of residence at Olney vicarage, where she in due course moved, wrote: "She had been used to a great deal of company, and we fearing that she would find such a transition into silent retirement irksome, contrived to give her our agreeable company often. Becoming continually more and more intimate, a practice obtained at length of our dining with each other alternately every day, Sundays excepted. In order to facilitate our communication, we made doors in the two garden walls..., by which means we considerably shortened the way from one house to the other, and could meet when we pleased without entering the town at all..."

Lady Austen was a high-spirited and a lively conversationalist. She quickly nurtured romantic designs upon Cowper which he, for the sake of keeping the peace with Mrs. Unwin, did not reciprocate, and was finally moved to write to William Unwin: "....at length having had repeated occasion to observe that she expressed a sort of romantic idea of our merits, and built such expectations of felicity upon our friendship, as we were sure that nothing human could possibly answer, I wrote to remind her that we were mortal, to recommend it to her not to think more highly of us than the subject would warrant.... ..." In short, he gave her the cold shoulder.

Mortally offended at this repulse, Lady Austen dashed off a letter so extreme that Cowper began to talk in his correspondence as if the relationship was finished. She had been "too much for us; occasionally perhaps it might refresh and revive us, but it more frequently exhausted us, neither your Mother nor I being in that respect at all a match for her." In the consequent mending of the breach Cowper rather enjoyed being the party to be wooed, finding himself in receipt of a gift of ruffles and a series of epistolary entreaties. It took until July 1782 and a theatrical, tearful embrace between Lady Austen and Mrs. Unwin before Cowper was prepared to renew the connection on former terms.

For the next eighteen months Lady Austen enjoyed the close company of Cowper, as previously described. Complaining about a lack of subject-matter one day, Cowper was told, "Oh, you can write upon any subject, write upon this Sofa." The sofa upon which Lady Austen sat, when making this remark, and therefore the ostensible subject of Cowper's next project, 'The Task', can be seen at Olney today--a diminutive article of furniture, by comparison with modern pieces of the same name. Having set him his task, Lady Austen did everything she could to obstruct its progress, keeping up her demands on her William's time. The two were once again on first-name terms, and now it was Cowper who appears to have developed a romantic attachment to his friend and Muse. The domestic atmosphere at Orchard Side turned sour. "Lady Austen's flow of spirits, and talent of ridicule, rendered their intercourse frequently uneasy, and always of precarious comfort or duration," wrote Samuel Greatheed.

By the autumn of 1784 it was over. Lady Austen had moved away for good. In July Cowper had written to Unwin, warning him, in case he ran into her in Bristol, where she had removed to visit a relation in Clifton, not to encourage any hope of rapprochement. (James King, throughout the episode of Cowper's involvement with Lady Austen, makes the confusing assumption that Clifton is a village within walking-distance of Olney). "If you should chance to fall into her company, remember if you please that we found the connexion on some accounts an inconvenient one; that we do not wish to renew it, and conduct yourself accordingly."

In one of the more eventful interludes in Cowper's letters-the intrusion of a political candidate and his entourage, during the spring campaign of 1784--the interest lies not so much in the action (the "mob" appearing at the window; the "smart rap" on the door; the maid's announcement; the party being led to the back of the house, because Puss, the hare was out of her box) as in the atmosphere which all this activity disrupts. "We were sitting yesterday after dinner, the two ladies and my self, very composedly, and without the least apprehension of any such intrusion in our snug parlour, one lady knitting, the other netting, and the gentleman winding worsted..." The picture tells us that what Cowper enjoyed most about his menage a trois was the sense of being one amongst the ladies. The charge of effeminacy has often been brought against him. It is not a charge, so much as an accurate representation of his own self-image. The intruding party, the outside world, is masculine and vigorous. A month earlier, with the country still in the grip of nine-week-long frost, he had written to Newton (from whom he was keeping the composition of 'the Task' a secret), blaming his forebears for the enfeeblement of the Cowper breed, "till at last the collected efforts of all their follies have centred in my puny self." In the same letter he spoke of seeing Adam in a dream. The first man was stocky, muscularly-built and filled with a rude animal energy. "Upon my hypothesis, therefore, there has been a gradual declension, in point of bodily vigour, from Adam down to me."

Before embarking on 'The Task', Cowper had taken a considerable amount of care over the translation of a group of thirty-seven poems, passed to him by William Bull, by the French Quietist, Madame Guyon. Jeanne-Marie Guyon (1648-1717) had written some of the poems while imprisoned in the Bastille between 1695 and 1702. After being widowed she had led an itinerant life, following the mystical teachings of Miguel de Molinos, an extreme Spanish Quietist, author of *Spiritual Guide* (1675), an influential seventeenth-century religious text. Molinos's teaching eliminated the need for the sacraments, arguing that the soul, given opportunity by a life of quietude and renunciation of self, could commune directly with God. Guyon described herself as the bride of Jesus, the "pregnant woman of the Apocalypse." The soul's desire to merge again with God became the central aspect of her own spiritual guides.

Cowper, so certain of his own exclusion, and the impossibility of his spiritual salvation, could not fail to be fascinated by a figure with an opposite sense of certainty. He mistrusted her extravagance, her fulsome childishness (which he tried accurately to replicate in his translations) but admired the lack of pride implicit in such faults. 'Self-Diffidence', 'The Necessity Of Self-Abasement' and 'Self-Love And Truth Incompatible' are examples of poems which must have influenced the translator as he worked on them.

A year before he began 'The Task', Cowper wrote out--tradition has it, in the course of a single night--'The Diverting History of John Gilpin', as told to him by Lady Austen. Not everyone finds this story of a man on a runaway horse humorous. I did, when it was first read to me as a ten-year-old, and I find children in that age-group still enjoy listening to it. It is a trifle, and only trifles of a certain quality are preserved. Initially, it seemed as if the squib would have only a temporary life. Cowper published it anonymously in the *Public Advertiser*, where it provoked little attention. But three years later a copy was put into the hands of an actor, Henderson, who included it in his one-man stage readings. Audiences were enthralled. Cowper was urged to write a continuation of the ballad, but never did, although in an edition of Hone's *Table Book* three verses are produced allegedly in Cowper's hand, and purporting to be a fragment of a companion-piece in which Mrs. Gilpin played the star-role.

Cowper considered he was doing something quintessentially British when writing 'John Gilpin'. "The ballad is a species of poetry," he wrote to William Unwin, in August 1783, "I believe peculiar to this country, equally adapted to the drollest, and the most tragical subjects. Simplicity and ease are its proper characteristics. Our forefathers excelled in it; but we moderns have lost the art. It is observed that we have few good English odes. But to make amends, we have many excellent ballads." There is, it has to be admitted, especially for today's taste, something geriatric about the humour in 'Gilpin'. It is partly a question of period. The practical, everyday mishaps of horsemanship were very much a live subject in the eighteenth century. They are not any more. Cowper himself put his finger on it when he wrote to William Unwin, saying, "Strange as it may seem, the most ludicrous lines I ever wrote have been written in the saddest mood, and but for that saddest mood, perhaps had never been written at all." The atmosphere of a story told to regale a flagging spirit does still hang about the poem.

4 THE TASK

An Advertisement printed at the front of the first edition of *The Task* read: "The history of the following production is briefly this: A lady, fond of blank verse, demanded a poem of that kind from the author, and gave him the SOFA for a subject. He obeyed; and, having much leisure, connected another subject with it; and, pursuing the train of thought to which his situation and turn of mind led him, brought forth at length, instead of the trifle which he at first intended, a serious affair--a Volume."

It was 'The Task' itself which proved the undoing of Lady Austen, for once engaged on it Cowper began to resent the time her company demanded. "We had seldom breakfasted ourselves till ten; and the intervening hour was all the time that I could find in the whole day for writing; and occasionally it would happen that the half of that hour was all that I could secure for the purpose," he later explained to his cousin, Lady Hesketh.

By the time Cowper came to embark upon his task he had arrived at a new sense of contentment. It was resigned and melancholic, but essentially he knew that his life had settled into the pattern for which it was intended. He wrote to Newton (still keeping the long poem a secret) in July 1783: "An invisible, uncontrollable agency, a local attachment, an inclination more forcible than I ever felt, even to the place of my birth, serves me for prison walls, and for bounds which I cannot pass... So it is, and it is so, because here is to be my abode, and because such is the appointment of Him that placed me in it... it is the place I love the most, not for any happiness it affords me, but because here I can be miserable with most convenience to myself, and with the least disturbance to others."

By the summer of 1784 he had completed the six books of 'The Task', but he waited until October, and it had gone to press, before telling Newton. Preceding letters had been dissembling, willfully elaborating on any matter (boyhood curiosity visits to Bedlam; opposition to Pitt's candle-tax; his attachment to the greenhouse) rather than the one he was nervous of revealing. "I mentioned it not sooner," he eventually steeled the courage to say, "because almost to the last I was doubtful I should ever bring it to a conclusion, working often in such distress of mind, as, while it spurred one to work, at the same time threatened to disqualify me for it." The next day he wrote to Unwin telling him the deed had been done. "He will be surprised, and perhaps not pleased. But I think he cannot complain, for he keeps his own authorly secrets..." Newton responded amicably enough, but Cowper read suppressed mortification between the lines and refused to send the proofs, as requested. Instead he posted off a copy of the title, headers and a short extract--all of which Newton found fault with.

There was again a delay of something like a year before the book was published, during which time other poems were added to the volume, some already written ('John Gilpin'), some new ('Tirocinium' and 'Epistle To Hill'). The stage success of Gilpin led to quick and dramatic sales. Soon a new edition was required, and such a quantity of fresh demand for Cowper's earlier book was created that in due course a double edition was issued. Almost overnight Cowper found himself the best-selling poet of his age. The critics were no less enthusiastic, although few of them remarked on its essential distinctiveness. As James King reports Wordsworth being amongst the first to recognize, "'The Task' was the first significant autobiographical narrative poem in the English language." Or, as Benham with characteristic straightforwardness puts it: "'The Task' is all about himself."

The six books are entitled The Sofa; The Time-Piece; The Garden; The Winter Evening; The Winter Morning Walk; The Winter Walk At Noon. It is predominantly a poem which celebrates domestic comfort in a crisp English winter setting. From this point of view it makes very cosy reading. And so it should. "I sing the sofa," is its defiant opening. That opening half-line cannot help but conjure up, to today's reader, an almost Whitmanesque braggadocio. It is certainly not the way we might expect a stricken-deer of a poet to begin.

The opening book sets out to tell a developmental history of the sofa, but Cowper deems this antiques-fair subject-matter worthy of a mere 100 lines. Prompted by the mention of gout he turns to singing the praises of physical exercise.

The Sofa suits
The gouty limb, 'tis true; but gouty limb,
Though on a Sofa, may I never feel:
For I have loved the rural walk through lanes
Of grassy swarth, close cropped by nibbling sheep
And skirted thick with intertexture firm
Of thorny boughs; have loved the rural walk
O'er hills, through valleys, and by rivers' brink,
E'er since a truant boy I passed my bounds
To enjoy a ramble on the banks of Thames;
And still remember, nor with regret,
Of hours that sorrow since has much endeared,
How oft, my slice of pocket store consumed,
Still hungering, penniless and far from home,
I fed on scarlet hips and stony haws,
Or blushing crabs, or berries that emboss
The bramble, black as jet, or sloes austere.
Hard fare! but such as boyish appetite
Disdains not, nor the palate undepraved
By culinary arts, unsavoury deems.
No Sofa then awaited my return,
Nor Sofa then I needed.

The greater part of this first book then becomes a sort of Cook's tour of the walks around Olney, their sights and sounds. The description is personal and circumstantial but, at the same time, ecological. After complaining about the felling of trees:

By ceaseless action all that is subsists.
Constant rotation of the unwearied wheel
That Nature rides upon, maintains her health,
Her beauty, her fertility. She dreads
An instant's pause, and lives but while she moves.
Its own resolvency upholds the world.
Winds from all quarters agitate the air,
And fit the limpid element for use,
Else noxious: oceans, rivers, lakes, and streams,
All feel the freshening impulse, and are cleansed
By restless undulation.
THE TASK I ll.367-377

There are those who might have responded that 'restless undulation' is exactly what Cowper sought to protect himself from in his private life. But although his life was quiet and uneventful, he would have argued that it was industrious. His criticism of gypsies was based on the parasitic nature of their life (see lines 557-591).

At the end of the first book Cowper turns to what will be a recurring and central theme--rural virtue versus metropolitan vice. "God made the country, and man made the town." He ends the book on an apocryphal note, no less defiant than his opening line. Society has become "A mutilated structure, soon to fall."

Book II, 'The Time-Piece', begins with "Reflections suggested by the conclusion of the former book." In other words the structure is arbitrary--from one point of view 'The Task' is a free-flowing sequence of reflections not easily ordered into a conventional epic structure. At this particular point in the poem, the reflections prompt a passionate plea for Britain to eradicate slavery from its colonies. "Spread it then/And let it circulate through every vein/Of all your empire; that where Britain's power/Is felt, mankind may feel his mercy too." (II ll.44-47)

As has been said before, Cowper was unflinching in his opposition to slavery and of those who can subjugate their fellow human beings just because they have a different-coloured skin. "He finds his fellow guilty of a skin/Not coloured like his own, and having power/To enforce the wrong, for such a worthy cause/Dooms and devotes him as his lawful prey." The language is animalistic, almost cannibalistic. We read back from 'prey' and 'devotes' transmutes into 'devours'. And yet had Cowper actually written 'devours' the effect would have been less. So strong were his feelings on this subject that for a long time he contemplated writing a poem specifically about the issue. In 1788 (by that time embroiled in his translation of Homer) he wrote to Lady Hesketh, "Slavery, or a release from slavery, such as the poor negroes have endured, or perhaps both these topics together, appeared to me a theme so important at the present juncture, and at the same time so perceptible of poetic management, that I have more than once perceived myself ready to start in that career." And he was somewhat put out when he heard that Hannah More - a poet and Christian moralist he much admired, thinking she had "more nerve and energy both in her thoughts and language than half the rhymers in the kingdom" - had beaten him to it. He did, as we have seen, eventually write three poems on this theme: 'The Negro's Complaint' ("Fleecy locks and black complexion/Cannot forfeit Nature's chain"); 'Pity For Poor Africans' (light and satirical, applying a parable about children plundering a neighbour's orchard); and 'The Morning Dream' (a vision of a goddess of righteousness going "to make freemen of slaves".) The first of these is the best, but none reaches the eloquence or subtlety of his lines in the early part of Book II of 'The Task'.

'The Time-Piece' opens with commentary on the bizarre behaviour in the elements and specifically on a recent earthquake in Sicily. Those who might like to make Cowper out to be a genial-minded fellow, by reference to the letters and some of his lighter verse, should be made to read the first 200 lines of this second book of 'The Task'. Here Cowper's belief in a vengeful deity, ever-watchful, and ever-ready, with finger on the button of divine reprisal, is given full expression. Rational explanations of natural disasters are scorned into oblivion:

Forth steps the spruce philosopher, and tells
Of homegeneal and discordant springs
And principles; of causes, how they work
By necessary laws their sure effects;
Of action and reaction. He has found
The source of the disease that nature feels,
And bids the world take heart and banish fear.
Thou fool! will thy discovery of the cause
Suspend the efect, or heal it? Has not God
Still wrought by means since first He made the world,
And did He not of old employ His means
To drown it? What is His creation less
Than a capacious reservoir of means
Formed for His use, and ready at His will?
THE TASK II ll.189-202

That "capacious reservoir of means/Formed for His use" becomes, on consideration, a terrifying concept. Cowper's own sense of terror, which was perpetual, had, therefore, a firm philosophical foundation. It was both an inducement and a springboard to his madness. Sanity in personal and public life could only be maintained by a sense of uprightness and moral rigor. When the land was governed well, by men of calibre and staunch heart, its residents could rest easier in their beds. That situation, Cowper felt, no longer existed in England. The country had just lost control of the American colonies. She had been humiliated on the high seas, double-crossed by France, and men of nobility such as Chatham and Wolfe (the conqueror of Quebec) were dead. The country was now governed by "effeminates", who hoped to repel a hostile force with nothing more robust than their "lavender" and "liquid sweets".

In this context, the men of the pulpit should be assuming the mantle of influence. Cowper treats the possibility with satire and sarcasm:

The things that mount the rostrum with a skip,
And then skip down again; pronounce a text,
Cry-hem! and reading what they never wrote,
Just fifteen minutes, huddle up their work,
And with a well-bred whisper close the scene!
THE TASK II ll.409-413

"I loathe all affectation. 'Tis my perfect scorn;/Object of my implacable disgust." This is heartfelt, and Cowper, keenly observant, is ready to catch it out, even in moments of relaxation. Although, when he wrote 'The Task', it had been several years since he had attended a church service, his memory of preachers' foibles remained vivid enough:

Some, decent in demeanour while they preach,
That task performed, relapse into themselves,
And having spoken wisely, at the close
Grow wanton, and give proof to every eye--
Whoe'er was edified, themselves were not.
Forth comes the pocket mirror. First we stroke
An eyebrow; next, compose a straggling lock;
Then with an air, most gracefully performed,
Fall back into our seat, extend an arm,
And lay it at its ease with gentle care,
With handkerchief in hand, depending low.
The better hand, more busy, gives the nose
Its bergamot, or aids the indebted eye
With opera-glass to watch the moving scene,
And recognize the slow retiring fair.
THE TASK II ll.440-454

Those enslaved to fashion and fortune, living uncomfortably beyond their means, are described as "so many maniacs dancing in their chains" and, in the mood he was in when writing this poem, Cowper clearly thought himself sane, and the world mad. If this second book is the least comfortable to read, and therefore the least popular section of 'The Task', it is because the strong views on his chosen subject-matter are held to more persistently than in the other books. There is less discursiveness, and no reference at all to the private world of the parlour or garden. His self-righteous mockery of men and women in every quarter culminates in a diatribe directed at school and college pedagogues who, by their pernicious influence (his brother is cited as a sole exception), are breeding a delusion which is spreading like the plague of frogs let loose in Egypt. "And the land stank, so numerous was the fry."

The general reader, coming to this book over two hundred years after it was written, is likely to recoil from the cantankerous peevishness on display. Cowper would no doubt argue that this is because the decadence he identified has continued through degenerate generation after generation. He might have approved of some aspects of the Victorian era, especially because he was in many ways that era's inspiration, but he would certainly have been alive to the hypocrisies at work. As far as his contemporary readers were concerned, Cowper appears to have been instinctively aware that the tone of the poem needed reining-in. "Now with pleasant pace a cleanlier road/I mean to tread," he says, near the beginning of 'The Garden'. But the mood, and mode, of condemnation are not so easy to shake off. After citing "Domestic happiness" in line 40, he slips into another long passage castigating various embodiments of hypocrisy. It is the infamous "stricken deer" conceit which draws Cowper back to his domestic theme.

> *I was a stricken deer that left the herd*
> *Long since; with many an arrow deep infixed*
> *My panting side was charged, when I withdrew*
> *To seek a tranquil death in distant shades."*
> *THE TASK III ll.108-111*

Lord David Cecil took this passage as the basis (and the title) for his 1929 biography, which has done much to distort the twentieth-century view of the poet. As Lodwick Hartley observes, in a bibliographical essay published in 1960, in Cecil's portrait "Cowper becomes a charming period-piece." And he dismisses the book as "essentially a refined piece of coddling, hardly satisfactory as more than entertainment."

It is another 200-odd lines before Cowper finally lets the hectoring tone drop; before he begins to praise the virtues of the good life, rather than denounce the vices of the bad. The essence of rural good living is its "silence and its shade". Cowper derides the "din of the swift pack,/And clamours of the field." Hunting is a "detested sport", from the clutches of which, he rejoices, his pet hare Puss has been safe for ten long years. And Cowper, in his domestic retreat, is much more like the "sheltered hare [who]/Has never heard the sanguinary yell/Of cruel man", than he is a stricken deer.

After a long passage detailing the pleasures and toils of gardening (pruning, cucumber-growing, compost-making, arranging bedding plants)--one of the finest treatments of the subject in English literature--Cowper ends the third book once again on the attack. England is in decline. "We have bid farewell/To all the virtues of those better days,/And all their honest pleasure." Those better days were when England remained predominantly a rural society, based on hereditary estates. Now "Estates are landscape, gazed upon a while,/Then advertised, and auctioneered away," to feed the hunger for city pleasures. Even where people choose to remain in the country it is so often in the style of that "omnipotent magician [Capability] Brown", to fashion their grounds in the latest style.

The lake in front becomes a lawn,
Woods vanish, hills subside, and valleys rise,
And streams, as if created for his use,
Pursue the track of his directing wand,
Sinuous or straight, now rapid and now slow,
Now murmuring soft, now roaring in cascades,
Even as he bids. The enraptured owner smiles.

'Tis finished! and yet, finished as it seems,
Still wants a grace, the loveliest it could show,
A mine to satisfy the enormous cost.
Drained to the last poor item of his wealth,
He sighs, departs, and leaves the accomplished plan
That he has touched, retouched, many a long day
Laboured, and many a long night pursued in dreams,
Just when it meets his hopes, and proves the heaven
He wanted, for a wealthier to enjoy.
THE TASK III ll.774-788

If this is a well-measured and surprisingly enduring exposure, Cowper roused himself to an even more sarcastic crescendo in the final 50 lines. London, in the winter season, becomes a "crowded coop" of "Ambition, avarice, penury incurred.By endless riot, vanity, the lust/Of pleasure...."

We are half-way through, with three books to go. In these three wintry books the pleasures of retreat do begin to predominate over sermonising vehemence. Less than 50 lines into 'The Winter Evening' we come upon the justly famous passage:

Now stir the fire, and close the shutters fast,
Let fall the curtains, wheel the sofa round,
And while the bubbling and loud hissing urn
Throws up a steamy column, and the cups
That cheer but not inebriate, wait on each,
So let us welcome peaceful evening in.
THE TASK IV ll.36-41

Cowper, learning of the fortunes of the world in a newspaper, feels the pleasure of an Olney detachment. Winter strengthens the impression:

I crown thee King of intimate delights,
Fireside enjoyments, homeborn happiness,
And all the comforts that the lowly roof
Of undisturbed retirement, and the hours

Of long uninterrupted evening know.
THE TASK IV ll.139-143

The opportunities for revery which early evenings afford are given wonderful expression in the following, exceptional passage:

Just when our drawing-rooms begin to blaze
With lights, by clear reflexion multiplied
From many a mirror, in which he of Gath,
Goliath, might have seen his bulk
Whole without stooping, towering crest and all,
My pleasures too begin. But me perhaps
The glowing hearth may satisfy awhile
With faint illumination, that uplifts
The shadow to the ceiling, there by fits
Dancing uncouthly to the quivering flame.
Not undelightful is an hour to me
So spent in parlour twilight; such a gloom
Suits well the thoughtful or unthinking mind,
The mind contemplative, with some new theme
Pregnant, or indisposed alike to all.
Laugh ye, who boast your more mercurial powers,
That never feel a stupor, know no pause,
Nor need one; I am conscious, and I confess,
Fearless, a soul that does not always think.
Me oft has fancy, ludicrous and wild,
Soothed with a waking dream of houses, towers,
Trees, churches, and strange visages expressed
In the red cinders, while with poring eye
I gazed, myself creating what I saw.
Nor less amused have I quiescent watched
The sooty films that play upon the bars
Pendulous, and foreboding, in the view
Of superstition, prophesying still,
Though still deceived, some stranger's near approach.
'Tis thus the understanding takes repose
In indolent vacuity of thought,
And sleeps and is refreshed. Meanwhile the face
Conceals the mood lethargic with a mask
Of deep deliberation, as the man
Were tasked to his full strength, absorbed and lost.

Thus oft, reclined at ease, I lose an hour
At evening, till at length the freezing blast,
That sweeps the bolted shutter, summons home
The recollected powers, and snapping short
The glassy threads with which the fancy weaves
Her brittle toils, restores me to myself.
How calm is my recess, and how the frost,
Raging abroad, and the rough wind, endear
The silence and the warmth enjoyed within!
THE TASK IV ll.267-310

What makes this exceptional is that never before had a poet spoken so directly, in the first-person, about processes of thought in this way. "Indolent vacuity of thought" has not previously been poetic subject-matter. The atmosphere of domestic revery quickly became the accepted territory of poetry (Coleridge's 'Frost At Midnight' was written in 1798), not because Cowper was a great experimentalist but, living so much within himself, he dared to be himself, rather than writing to a prevailing formula.

Cowper chose to centre so much of his description of domestic life in the season of winter because he knew that, writing when he did, the reveries he described reflected a luxury of the body as well as of the mind. For the poor the struggle to keep warm was a real one. He tells of a typical family, unable to have more than a brief blaze in the hearth, retiring to bed early ("Sleep seems their only refuge"), with all the food they possess "the brown loaf/Lodged on the shelf, half-eaten."

They live, and live without extorted alms
From grudging hands, but other boast have none
To soothe their honest pride, that scorns to beg;
Nor comfort else, but in their mutual love.
I praise you much, ye meek and patient pair,
For ye are worthy; choosing rather far
A dry but independent crust, hard earned,
And eaten with a sigh, than to endure

The rugged frowns and insolent rebuffs
Of knaves in office, partial in the work
Of distribution;
THE TASK IV ll.403-413

Cowper is always on the side of self-reliance. (He would have been very at home amongst the American Transcententalists.) His loathing of "laziness or sottish waste" is given vent in a way which reveals that he had little self-consciousness (perhaps it was a blind spot) about the parasitic basis of his own personal life. But whether writing about virtue or vice, one of the pleasures of reading 'The Task' is its presentation of circumstantial detail. Some would have us believe that the theft of garden equipment and furniture is a recent trend. Not so. Cowper writes of what a typical nocturnal thief of the eighteenth century had in view:

Woe to the gardener's pale, the farmer's hedge
Plashed neatly, and secured with driven stakes
Deep in the loamy bank. Uptorn by strength,
Resistless in so bad a cause, but lame
To better deeds, he bundles up the spoil,
An ass's burden, and when laden most
And heaviest, light of foot steals fast away.
THE TASK IV ll.436-442

The later part of 'The Winter Evening' is a lament for a lost country lifestyle, now corrupted by the influence of the town. "The town has tinged the country; and the stain/Appears a spot upon a vestal's robe,/The worse for what it soils." Dairy maids strut about in high heels, their hair done up in the latest fashion; householders have to lock their doors, especially at night; a walk in the woods is become a matter of anxiety.

Cowper turns sociologist and lays the severest blame for this "lamented change...from good to ill,/From ill to worse," at the door of mass conscription to the armed services. Here, because he is simply arguing, and not satirising, he becomes uncharacteristically inept and bumbling. Even if intended, the repetition in the following lines is ungainly: "By slow degrees,/Unapt to learn, and formed of stubborn stuff,/He yet by slow degrees puts off himself,/Grows conscious of a change, and likes it well." The soldier returns home and "hates the field in which no fife or drum/Attends him." He has become "a pest, where he was useful once."

At the close of this book Cowper returns to speaking more directly in the first person, and owns to admiration for Abraham Cowley, whose retirement, in later life, at Chertsey, was something of a model for his own withdrawal from the world. Like Cowper, Cowley had gone to Westminster school, and one of the earliest Cowper letters (written, when he was nineteen, to his friend Chase Price) indicates that Cowley's Pindaric odes were particular favourites. And in the accompanying poem, composed in response to news of the death of their mutual acquaintance, Cyril Arthington, Cowper invokes: "Come Heavenly Muse who Cowley's Bosom fired/His Judgment Strengthen'd and his Wit inspired/Explore the Secrets of my Mind."

In reading 'The Task' we slip in and out of the Cowper mind, but even when looking out, we are looking with his own observant eye. It is evident that his rural reveries were reserved for indoors, beside the fire. When he was outdoors, his head was up, eyes alert and watchful. He noticed ways and habits rather than the details of nature. Nearly all of his country description is concerned with the interplay of human or animal life with the landscape. He sees a man walking a dog. All his attention is fixed upon the behaviour of the pet. "Close behind his heel/Now creeps he slow; and now with many a frisk/Wide scampering, snatches up the drifted snow/With ivory teeth, or ploughs it with his snout;/Then shakes his powdered coat and barks for joy." Reading these lines four or five times over gives an effect like watching a video-grab on loop replay.

A long middle section in 'The Winter Morning Walk' concerns more public themes--monarchy, national identity, oppression, enslavement. Cowper's obsession with the principle of freedom arose from his consciousness of a divine ensnarement. He, a prisoner of his own damnation, could not bear to see men and women made slaves on earth.

That man should thus encroach on fellow-man,
Abridge him of his just and native rights,
Eradicate him, tear him from his hold
Upon the endearments of domestic life
And social, nip his fruitfulness and use,
And doom him for perhaps a heedless word
To barrenness, and solitude, and tears,
Moves indignation, makes the name of king
(Of king whom such prerogative can please)
As dreadful as the Manichean God,
Adored through fear, strong only to destroy.
THE TASK V ll.435-445

Although Cowper was not a Manichean, he did, if only in his periods of depression, consider himself as doomed as any slave or prisoner.

"The age of virtuous politics is past,/And we are deep in that of cold pretence..." ushers in another long digression on hypocrisy. "Conduct hath the loudest tongue," and a profession of faith and moral rectitude is belied by actions.

The last 350 lines of this penultimate book find Cowper writing as the advocate of religious wonder and contentment. It does have to be admitted that he is not as strong on advocacy as on satire. It beckons him into a formalistic style of metaphor and simile which is not his natural voice. Only when he has returned to specific observation, as in the beginning of Book VI, 'The Winter Walk At Noon', that (in this case, while describing a walk in snowy fields) the striking little saws that became the proverbial talismans for so many Victorian Christians, are created. "Knowledge is proud that he has learned so much;/Wisdom is humble that he knows no more." "Nature is but a name for an effect/Where cause is God."

The story of Misagathus and Evander is a strange intrusion. Benham's Notes to the Globe edition call it "disagreeable and very improbable". But Cowper's purpose in telling it is very clear (and plainly advertised in the ten lines which precede its telling), arising, as it did, out of his love and regard for animals. His attitude towards them is as plain as it could possibly be.

I would not enter on my list of friends
(Though graced with polished manners and fine sense,
Yet wanting sensibility) the man
Who needlessly sets foot upon a worm.
An inadvertent step may crush the snail
That crawls at evening in the public path;
But he that has humanity, forewarned,
Will tread aside, and let the reptile live.
The creeping vermin, loathsome to the sight,
And charged perhaps with venom, that intrudes,
A visitor unwelcome, into scenes
Sacred to neatness and repose, the alcove,
The chamber, or refectory, may die...
THE TASK VI ll.560-572

This is the unsentimental gardener speaking, who has no compunction in protecting his plants from infestation, by any means. Sensing that his praise of nature and defense of animal life require self-justification, Cowper lets rip with a sustained attack on the vogue for hero-worship and crowd adulation. The passage ("Man praises man..." ll.664-728) is too long to quote. More interesting is the rather smug tone with which Cowper chooses to bring his 'Task' to a close. In the passage beginning "He is the happy man..." (line 906), delineating the virtues of a retiring life of unassuming habit, Cowper disguises, in the third person, a flattering self-portrait. Although the sighing "So glide my life away!" of line 1000 is intended to carry a tone of "If only I might live my life in such a way", the actual effect of the word "so" is to convert the meaning to "Just so glides my life away"(and what a good life it is too!).

Some commentators have found these closing lines self-consoling. They read to me more like self-congratulation. "The voice is that of a man assured within himself," says Vincent Newey. But it is a self-assurance not unperturbed by the lack of attention from a "self-approving naughty world". Of course, in a trite sense, every poet publishing is saying, "Take notice, take notice." But in some poems this is underwritten in the very fabric of the verse. It is in Tennyson's 'In Memoriam', which is self-pleading towards both its personal audience (Emily) and the public. And it is in Cowper's 'The Task'. Having, after a slow beginning, written with speed and fluency, Cowper had arrived at a new self-image as a writer. If he could write to Unwin about this time, "I have no more right to the name of poet, than a maker of mouse-traps has to that of an engineer," it was in the tone of a disarming if disingenuous modesty. Disingenuousness pursued--"such a talent in verse as mine, is like a child's rattle, very entertaining to the trifler that uses it, and very disagreeable to all beside"--tips insincerity into immodesty.

5 LIFE-NOTES (III)

In finding a new self-image, Cowper had to cast off an old one, and ended, literally, casting off the life that had been Olney. In May, 1784, he and Mrs. Unwin attended a balloon launch at Weston Underwood, in the grounds of the Throckmortons, a Catholic family held at arms-length by most people in Olney. Cowper himself had long enjoyed the freedom to roam at will on their estate, but this attendance at a public event heralded a closer acquaintance with the people he came to call Mr. and Mrs. Frog.

The success of 'The Task' had the effect of renewing contact with one of his cousins, Harriot Hesketh, who wrote to him out of the blue. She (now Lady Hesketh, and a widow, her husband having died in 1782) offered Cowper financial support, which he did not hesitate to accept. "Whensoever and whatsoever, and in what manner soever you please," he encouraged and, in a manner reminiscent of Lady Austen's assault on Orchard Side, Lady Hesketh was soon visiting Olney and staying at the Vicarage. He had wanted to accommodate her at Orchard Side, giving up his study for the purpose, but this proposal was vetoed by Mrs. Unwin, who made arrangements to acquire an apartment on the opposite side of the square. In the end, it was the Vicarage.

As a result of this renewed family contact, Cowper found himself suddenly £100 a year the richer. £20 came directly from Lady Hesketh, £20 from Lord Cowper, £10 from another relative, but the lion's share, £50, was from an anonymous benefactor, believed to have been Theadora. It was also Lady Hesketh who urged a change of scene upon Cowper. The Throckmortons had a vacant lodge on their estate; it was offered on very reasonable terms; and Cowper and Mrs. Unwin moved out of Orchard Side in November 1786. A month or two earlier Cowper had written to William Unwin elaborating the arguments in favour of a move: "Here we have no neighbourhood, there we shall have most agreeable neighbours in the Throckmortons. Here we have a bad air in winter, impregnated with the fishy smelling fumes of the marsh miasma; there we shall breathe in an atmosphere untainted. Here we are confined from September to March, and sometimes longer; there we shall be upon the very verge of pleasure-grounds in which we can always ramble, and shall not wade through almost impassable dirt to get at them."

One person remained unconvinced. Cowper's coming out into the world - with his publication of the 'The Task' and his renewed family contact - was looked at askance by Newton, who saw the first dozen years at Olney being undermined. Cowper's very soul was in danger of being lost--the more so, because he had now made friends with Catholics. In September he fired off a warning to Cowper, telling him that any sinful behaviour would be reported on by his spies in Olney.

A fortnight after the move, Mrs. Unwin's son, William died, of typhoid fever. Cowper took the loss of his friend and correspondent badly, but does not appear to have read it as a sign that an ill star hung over his change of circumstance. He continued to rejoice in his new, spacious abode, and in December wrote to Hill: "I cannot give you a better idea of what we have left, than by telling you the present candidates for it are a publican and a shoemaker." In the New Year Unwin's place in Cowper's life was filled by a twenty-year-old student, Samuel Rose, who called in en route from Glasgow to London, bearing regards from some Scottish academics, and a gift of Burns's poems.

During the first six months of 1787 Cowper became suicidally depressed. He lost weight and ceased his correspondence. It was reported later that Mrs. Unwin herself had had to cut the rope with which Cowper tried to hang himself. By the summer he was well enough to renew his correspondence, but he was left with a perpetual ringing in his ears and, more commodious as Weston Lodge might be, it was never to be the scene of the type of ordered contentment that had been found in Olney. In that degree, Newton's analysis was wise before the event.

The friendship with Sam Rose (who was later to be the legal representative of Blake, at his trial in 1803) developed well. The years at Weston, which continued until 1791, were consumed, as far as poetry was concerned, with the continuing translation of Homer. Benham's attitude to this work has been typical of all subsequent estimates of this endeavour: "It seems to me dreary and dull, but not more so than other translations of Homer. He was qualified by his scholarship, which Pope was not. The translation, therefore, is probably as accurate as any translation can be. But he had no sympathy for the wars and battles... His undertaking it at all seems to me one of the misfortunes arising from the breach with Lady Austen. She might have suggested something better than the wasting of five years in such profitless labour."

A longer study of Cowper would certainly need to take stock of this viewpoint. James King's chapters on Homer are the most valuable sections in his biography, but they do not attempt to be evaluative. There is no room here to do anything other than let Cowper defend himself against the accusation of plainness. "I reply beforehand," he wrote in the preface, "that I know it--that it would be absurd were it otherwise, and that Homer himself stands in the same predicament."

If Cowper could also speak in terms of his work as therapy, his most effective therapy always came in the form of practical employment. At Olney it had been his gardening and his amateur woodworking. At Weston he turned to path-laying. "I am making a gravel path"--he announced in a letter to Lady Hesketh, written in September 1787--"for winter use under a warm hedge in the orchard. It shall be furnished with a low seat for your accommodation, and if you do but like it I shall be gratified." As for exercise, Cowper was always more of a stroller than a serious walker. In May 1788 he walked to Gayhurst, described as a 55-minute walk, and remarked that it had been "A longer journey than I have walked on foot these seventeen years." Since losing his pet hares, he now kept a small spaniel named Beau (acquired through the good offices of the daughters of Sir Robert Gunning, retired diplomat), who accompanied him on his walks. In August he wrote to Lady Hesketh describing how the dog had swum into the Ouse to fetch a water-lily which he had earlier tried, and failed, to reach with his cane. The incident was immediately turned into a poem, 'The Dog And The Water-Lily'.

In 1786, the year of his move to Weston, he composed for Lady Hesketh a poem called 'Gratitude', in which he thanked her for all her generosity. The list of articles for which he and Mary Unwin have Lady Hesketh to thank--wheel-footed studying chair, carpets, table, mirror, bookshelves, china, curtains--leaves the reader wondering at the genteel poverty in which they must have lived before her arrival. What pleasure these new possessions and his new house brought Cowper was short-lived. Mrs. Unwin began to age and suffered a series of strokes which left her progressively disabled. When Hayley visited them in the summer of 1792, he reported a crude attempt to spark her back to life by means of shock-therapy, administered by the aptly-named local man, Mr. Socket. "We think it has been of material service," Cowper wrote to Lady Hesketh. But it was wishful thinking. He had already, in effect, lost his life-companion, and his own declining years were beginning.

He started to hear voices and went to the trouble of having them transcribed and interpreted by a local schoolmaster, Samuel Teedon. Mrs. Unwin began talking gibberish and having fits of inexplicable laughter. His voices, and her rantings were, for long periods, the only society he enjoyed. Eventually, Lady Hesketh (whose own health was now poor) advised a complete change of scene, and it was decided that the pair of them should move to Norfolk, where John Johnson was prepared to arrange dwellings and act as guardian.

They left Weston on Tuesday, July 28th, 1795. Mrs. Unwin lasted only a few months. After her death, Cowper was taken in by Johnson, who arranged to have a hole cut in the wall of the guest bedroom where Cowper slept, through which a tin tube was inserted, for the conveyance of artificially transmitted messages, designed to drown out the darker voices. It was a bizarre and useless scheme.

Cowper declined into a depressed dotage, refusing to speak to those who took the trouble to visit him and surviving on a diet of bread dunked in a daily bottle of port. He died just before five in the afternoon on August 25th, 1800. His only work during his last years had been annotations for his translation of Homer, and for a proposed new edition of Milton. A little over a year before he died, on successive days, he wrote 'On The Ice Islands' and 'The Castaway'. The first of these is little-known. It concerns a large ice-mass reported floating in the 'German ocean', i.e. the North Sea.

What portents, from what distant region, ride
Unseen till now in ours, the astonished tide?

Cowper, who had always been terrified of any mountainous bulk (he had even felt intimidated by the South Downs, in his previous venture out of Buckinghamshire--a visit to Hayley in Sussex), here identifies with the frosty crags, daring to float into warmer currents. He summons them back to their proper place.

Seek your home, nor longer rashly dare
The darts of Phoebus, and a softer air;
Lest ye regret, too late, your native coast,
In no congenial gulf for ever lost!

This notion of an object driven loose from its own climate seems to have sparked off the idea for 'The Castaway', a poem which, although very different in mood, bears comparison with Tennyson's 'Crossing The Bar'. Both became huge favourites with the general reader. Both seemed to sum up the poet's dying mood. Both were written in a sudden inspiration, at a single sitting. Both carry complete conviction--Tennyson's of salvation and safety in the afterlife, Cowper's of perdition. 'The Castaway' is an awesome and terrible final testament--proof that Cowper went to the grave convinced that he had been shunned by God.

Wise in this regard, and intermittently horribly disturbed by it, he had controlled the tenor of his life as best he could. There had been method in his attachment to Mary Unwin; method in his handling of Lady Austen and Lady Hesketh, and method in his connection to the rich Throckmortons. I would not want to suggest that there was not proper regard and affection as well, but they were all relationships which had the added attraction of material benefit. There had been madness in his rejection of Theadora, a madness born of his inclination to lead a life of dependency.

Although he has not been much studied in the second half of the twentieth century, much of Cowper's poetry has remained in the general reader's canon. Shorter poems as diverse as 'The Castaway', 'John Gilpin' and 'The Colubriad' are still frequently read. The longer poems are turned to less often. 'The Task' is dipped into and rarely read complete. The Moral Satires are held at arms-length, owing to a misrepresentation of their actual quality.

6 THE SHORTER VERSE & LETTERS

Since this short study aims to be both a guide and an inducement to a reading of the less popular as well as the better known of Cowper's poems -- the absence of a full and lively study of Cowper the poet becomes increasingly shameful as we approach the bicentenary of his death--the letters are left to speak for themselves. The high reputation enjoyed by Cowper's correspondence is fully justified, but it has sometimes been allowed to overshadow his standing as a poet. The letters of Byron and Keats would still be worth reading, even if some quirk of publishing history had resulted in the loss of all their poems. The same is pre-eminently true of Cowper. But it has to be acknowledged that there is a more intricate equivalence and relationship between the literary (as opposed to the biographical) character of the letters and the verse in Cowper's case. There is rather more of Cowper's correspondence that we would be reluctant to trade in exchange for the poems than is the case with either Keats or Byron. Admirers of their work would probably be willing to sacrifice all of the correspondence in exchange for a single poem. But, presented with a straight choice between 'The Task' and the letters, many of Cowper's most avid readers would be confronted with a more agonising decision. It would be dishonest not to acknowledge that this is so. It is partly because the personality of the man is so endearingly communicated in his letters. And also because so much of the subject matter covered in the poetry, is given another, more informal angle in the prose. Most of what Cowper said in his poems, he said also, in another form, in the letters.

The best-known example of a direct correspondence between letters and verse is 'The Colubriad', Cowper's tale of an encounter with a garden snake. The original version of this story is contained in a letter to William Unwin dated August 3, 1782, a time when Cowper was translating the poems of Madame Guyon, and looking forward to the arrival at the Vicarage of Lady Austen. He was aware that his life was passing through a period of happy placidity. "It is a sort of paradise, but it is true: we are never more in danger than when we think ourselves most secure, nor in reality more secure, than when we seem to be most in danger," he wrote to William Unwin. And then, by way almost of a parable to teach himself to remain ever vigilant, he tells Unwin how he has, "by an act of decapitation...not immediately mortal" with a garden hoe, rid his garden of a serpent. Extricated from the context of the letter, as in the eventual poetic version of the story, the ominous import of the snake, apart from the actual danger it represents to the three kittens, is lost, and it is part of the poem's charm that Cowper does not add--as he does, for example, in 'The Retired Cat'--an explanatory moral, despite having one ready to hand. The only poetic license taken in recounting the story is that Cowper allows himself to, apparently, fell the viper with a single blow:

And fearing every moment he would bite,
And rob our household of our only cat
That was of age to combat with a rat,
With outstretched hoe I slew him at the door,
And taught him NEVER TO COME THERE NO MORE.

'The Retired Cat' is similarly written up from a true incident. It concerns a cat finding a comfortable spot in an open drawer in a bedroom chest, only to have the drawer shut fast by an officious chambermaid. Cowper is no longer well-known for these flights of whimsy, although even his first volume contained the 'Report Of An Ajudged Case (Not To Be Found In Any Of The Books)', in which the Nose and the Eye contend for pride of place.

Between Nose and Eyes a strange contest arose,
The spectacles set them unhappily wrong;
The point in dispute was, as all the world knows,
To which the said spectacles ought to belong.

Unlike this poem, much of his shorter verse was only published posthumously and originally composed for the private entertainment of Mrs. Unwin and his correspondents. Not so 'Verses Supposed To Be Written By Alexander Selkirk' which found its way into a 1787 edition of the Scots Magazine, presented as the genuine article, a product of Selkirk's own pen.

"How fleet is a glance of the mind!" The speed and agility of the human mind intrigued Cowper. Locke (1632-1704) had defined an idea as "whatsoever is the Object of the Understanding when a Man thinks," or "Whatever it is which the Mind can be employ'd about thinking." The range and power of such a concept of Mind lies behind Selkirk's opening declaration, "I am monarch of all I survey", but it is a power, a regality, presented as cold and inhumane. "I am out of humanity's reach," and although imagination (not invoked in the romantic manner, but simply conceived as straightforward thinking or contemplation) has the ability to conjure up pictures of home, the transportation is soon brought to heel by the here and now. "But alas! recollection at hand/Soon hurries me back to despair." The poem is a short dramatic monologue, and one which carries complete conviction, but for today's reader the autobiographical, confessional undertones have rather undermined the historical context.

The here and now is not a hard and fast reality but an apprehension affected by disposition. This is articulated in 'The Shrubbery', originally titled 'The Spinny'. The poem is subtitled 'Written In A Time Of Affliction', and scenes, once the arena of happy experiences and still associated with them in the memory, are represented as being much more closely tied to present anguish than to past bliss.

O happy shades! to me unblest!
Friendly to peace, but not to me!
How ill the scene that offers rest,
And heart that cannot rest agree!

This short, six-verse poem is frightening in its representation of the tyranny of misery--"...fixed unalterable Care...slights the season and the scene." It carries a message of rebuke to those who would encourage the depressed to pay curative visits to pleasant landscapes. Cowper's view of the supremacy of mind is modern and sophisticated when compared with the notion that a stroll in the open-air could be a cure-all for any sickliness of thought.

In an amendment to the original ending of the much jauntier 'The Poplar Field', Cowper wrote:

The change both my heart and my fancy employs,
I reflect on the frailty of man and his joys;
Short-lived as we are, yet our pleasures, we see,
Have a still shorter date, and die sooner than we.

When I was at school I had a bald-headed teacher, nicknamed the Mekon (after the dome-headed villain from Venus, Dan Dare's arch enemy in the weekly comic, the *Eagle*), for whom the only way of reading Keats was to filter everything through the word transience. We transcribed the word in our notes more than once every lesson. Although we never took to this teacher, he did have his merits. He was methodical, paced the course well, and ensured that even the weakest in the group obtained a reasonable grade in the exam. But we preferred his colleague, a man who taught us Byron and Walter Scott, had no fixed agenda, and was easily persuaded to talk about all and sundry matters unrelated to the text. The Mekon had a genuine response to the poetry of Keats, but he was reading it with a middle-aged perspective. He spoke to us about pleasures that did not last, fruit that died on the vine. Keats was transfixed by intimations of his own mortality. He had genuine cause for his heightened state of anxiety. But late adolescence is a time when many feel overcome by a morbid hypochondria and convince themselves that the life-coil hangs by a thread. It is an obvious point, but you don't have to be suffering from tuberculosis to appreciate Keats.

Nor do you need to be a manic depressive to appreciate Cowper.

But he is a difficult poet for the young to get a handle on. The Mekon, I surmise, would have been an excellent interpreter of Cowper. He would have used 'The Poplar Field' as an emblem of the endemic transience of all things in the world. Some wit in the class might have compared the felling of the poplars with the loss of the Mekon's hair.

The poplars are felled; farewell to the shade,
And the whispering sound of the cool colonnade
The winds play no longer and sing in the leaves,
Nor Ouse on his bosom their image receives.

In this poem Cowper is responding to a landscape utterly altered across a twelve year timescale. It is not just the trees that have fallen. The spirit of place, represented by pleasant memories, has also fled. Its passing (the trees once tall and erect, are now supine, dead trunks, lying in the long grass as memorials of their former presence) encourages intimation of mortality:

My fugitive years are all hasting away,
And I must ere long lie as lowly as they,
With a turf on my breast and a stone at my head,
Ere another such grove shall arise in its stead.

Young poets sometimes write in this vein, but usually in a manner of vaunting borrowed robes. The changing landscape does not normally affect us in this way before mid-life. I was nineteen when I first read Cowper, and I turned to him intermittently throughout my twenties, but it was always with the feeling that I was missing a great deal. This has turned out to be a straightforward accumulation of years. Very little other baggage stands between Cowper and his reader. He does not use complicated diction, has (mostly) no axe to grind, and his versification is conventional.

Cowper, it has to be confessed, is a downbeat poet. Nearly everything he wrote was expressive of a disappointment that life in this world held no great joyous experiences in store. Promises of delight on earth were never realised. And so he sang (and wrote in his letters) of simple pleasures and diversions. Once again, this is the voice of mid-to-late-life. When he was sixty he was sent a picture of his mother, and wrote 'On The Receipt Of My Mother's Picture Out Of Norfolk'. In this poem, which is made beautiful by its understated but irrefutable emotion, Cowper talks of the promises he was given, as a young child, that his mother would one day return to earth. In his infant way, he took such promises literally, and the very real disappointment they gave rise to is seen as seeping through the entirety of his life:

What ardently I wished I long believed,
And, disappointed still, was still deceived,
By expectation every day beguiled,
Dupe of to-morrow even from a child.
Thus many a sad to-morrow came and went,
Till, all my stock of infant sorrow spent,
I learnt at last submission to my lot...

The middle section of this poem attempts to contain circumstantial memories of his mother, but these are--not surprisingly, considering how young Cowper was when she died--somewhat thin. He remembers her "nightly visits to my chamber", her washing his face, his own playing with the tissued ornaments on her dress. The conclusion is shot through with an ambivalent attitude towards the imagination.

And, while the wings of Fancy still are free,
And I can view this mimic show of thee,
Time has but half succeeded in his theft--
Thyself removed, thy power to soothe me left.

Although the final word is intended to carry the meaning "remains", it cannot help but also suggest "departed", "fled". If Time has only "but half succeeded", the imagination's success has also been less than convincing.

There are those--Cowper's biographer, James King, is one--who make too much of Cowper's mother's death. For them this poem is a marvellous testimony to Cowper's appreciation of his mother. Viewed critically and unsentimentally, the poem is considerably weakened by being twenty or so lines too long. A dozen lines are spent in building an inappropriate Virgilian conceit, comparing his mother with a British cargo boat at last finding its haven in an exotic port. This ushers in a familiar, self-pitying self-representation:

But me, scarce hoping to attain that rest,
Always from port withheld, always distressed--
Me howling blasts drive devious, tempest tost,
Sails ripped, seams opening wide, and compass lost,
And day by day some current's thwarting force
Sets me more distant from a prosperous course.

The facts of Cowper's domestic seclusion, and the "stricken deer" metaphor--which, once taken up by Sir David Cecil, has taken hold in an exaggerated way--have rather obscured the obvious. Cowper felt himself morally and spiritually at sea, extremely vulnerable and exposed, out in the unsheltered dark.

One of his most popular Olney hymns, 'Oh For A Closer Walk With God', which was written in 1767, while Mrs. Unwin was seriously ill, calls, in its second line, for "A calm and heavenly frame." After writing that second line, Cowper fell asleep. "When I awaked again the third and fourth were whisper'd to my Heart in a way which I have often experienced." This confession aligns Cowper with other somnial poets, such as Blake and Coleridge. The third and fourth lines referred to--'A light to shine upon the road/That leads me to the Lamb!'--even have something about them of Blake's *Songs of Innocence.*

'God Moves In A Mysterious Way', composed during a solitary walk, is a very fine, concise poem. Given a sprinkling of dashes, in place of commas and semi-colons, it might pass for the work of Emily

Dickinson, so condensed and vivid is its imagery. Clouds "Are big with mercy, and shall break/In blessings on your head." The final verse has about it the sort of directness which mocks interpretation.

Blind unbelief is sure to err,
And scan his work in vain:
God is his own interpreter,
And He will make it plain.

Sometimes in the hymns Cowper is too full of Calvinistic disdain for the unelect. 'The Narrow Way' depicts faith as a minority privilege. "None but the chosen tribes of God/Will seek or choose it for their own." And this hymn ends with a finger-wagging "Cleave to the world, ye sordid worms,/Contented lick your native dust!" Cowper is infinitely more sympathetic when considering his own wormliness, as in 'When darkness long has veiled my mind".

Oh! let me then at length be taught
What I am still so slow to learn;
That God is Love, and changes not,
Nor knows the shadow of a turn.

Sweet truth, and easy to repeat!
But when my faith is sharply tried,
I find myself a learner yet,
Unskilful, weak, and apt to slide.

But, O my Lord, one look from thee
Subdues the disobedient will,
Drives doubt and discontent away,
And thy rebellious worm is still.

God's love, in Cowper's case, took the human form of Mary Unwin. She was his angel in the house, ministering to his discontent. His beautiful tribute to her, 'To Mary', written in the autumn of 1793, is shot through with a sense of responsibility for burdening her with so much depression.

The twentieth year is well-nigh past,
Since first our sky was overcast;
Ah, would that this might be the last!
My Mary!

Thy spirits have a fainter flow,
I see thee daily weaker grow;
'Twas my distress that brought thee low,
My Mary!

There are thirteen such verses in the poem, each one ending in the same exclamation. Although Mary had remained Mary Unwin to the last, this poem makes clear that Cowper had loved her. It is also one of the finest poems written by one partner for another in old age. It is very much a poem of decrepitude, in which the reader encounters image after image of physical decline. And Time (or transience) is not seen as the sole or even principle cause. Cowper blames himself.

But ah! by constant heed I know,
How oft the sadness that I show
Transforms thy smiles to looks of woe,
My Mary!

And should my future lot be cast
With much resemblance of the past,
Thy worn-out heart will break at last,
My Mary!

At the time of writing this poem, Cowper had been made hyper-sensitive to the likelihood of losing Mary, not just by her very real frailty, but also by an exchange of letters with the Rev. James Hurdis, author of 'The Village Curate' and vicar of Bishopstone in Sussex. Hurdis's favourite sister, Catherine, had died in 1792, and much of his correspondence had consisted in lengthy tributes to her. Cowper, when writing 'To Mary', had recently supported Hurdis in his successful bid to become Professor of Poetry at Oxford.

In the main, in later life, Cowper saved his humour and sense of irony for his letters. The ability to be effectively satirical about himself, as in the early 'An Ode', needs to be more forcefully acknowledged as one of Cowper's attributes:

Shall I begin with Ah, or Oh?
Be sad? Oh! yes. Be glad? Ah! no.
Light subjects suit not grave Pindaric ode,
Which walks in metre down the Strophic road.
But let the sober matron wear
Her own mechanic sober air:
Ah me! ill suits, alas! the sprightly jig... ...

The rest of this early poem elucidates the young Cowper's opposition to poetic posing in "Smooth, soothing sounds, and sweet alternate time,/Clinking, like change of bells, in tingle tangle chime."

Cowper's characteristic morbidity was already evident in the 'Delia' poems, that curious sequence of poems which arose from his early love affair with his cousin, and which are at the same time the work of a very different and a very similar character. They are jaunty as the older poet was not. But the underlying tone is at one with the later work. Here is the opening to 'Written After Leaving Her At New Burns', one of several poems composed after quarrels or partings:

How quick the change from joy to woe!
How chequered is our lot below!
Seldom we view the prospect fair,
Dark clouds of sorrow, pain, and care
(Some pleasing intervals between)
Scowl over more than half the scene.

Forced to part from his cousin after a five-day togetherness, he is left with just her verbal assurance of her continuing regard for him.

And can I doubt, my charming maid,
As unsincere what you have said?

Banished from thee to what I hate,
Dull neighbours and insipid chat,
No joy to cheer me, none in view,
But the dear hope of meeting you;
And that through passion's optic scene,
With ages interposed between;
Blessed with the kind support you give,
'Tis by your promised truth I live;
How deep my woes, how fierce my flame,
You best may tell who feel the same.

By all accounts Delia, or Theadora as she really was, remained true to her first love. She never married, and anonymously provided Cowper (who, when he wrote the line "Blessed with the kind support you give", was certainly not thinking of money) with financial support throughout his life.

SELECT BIBLIOGRAPHY

Poems and Letters

Scholarly editions of Cowper's poems and letters have only become available since 1980. The following are published by the Clarendon Press, Oxford:

The Letters and Prose Writings edited by James King and Charles Ryskamp 5 vols.

The Poems (only the 1st. volume has so far been published)

Books about Cowper:

Lord David Cecil *The Stricken Deer* (1929)

Lodwick Hartley *William Cowper, the Continuing Revaluation* (1960)

William Hayley *The Life and Letters Of William Cowper Esq.* (1809)

James King *William Cowper, A Biography* (1986)

Vincent Newey *Cowper's Poetry* (1982)

Norman Nicholson *William Cowper* (1951)

Charles Ryskamp *William Cowper of the Inner Temple Esq.* (1959)

Gilbert Thomas *William Cowper and the Eighteenth Century* (1935)

Indispensable Essays about Cowper:

Virginia Woolf: "Cowper And Lady Austen" in The Second Common Reader, 1932

Kenneth MacLean: "William Cowper" in The Age of Johnson ed. Frederick Hilles, 1949

D. J. Enright: "William Cowper" in Pelican Guide To English Literature from Dryden to Johnson, 1957

Donald Davie: The Critical Principle 2 William Cowper in the Cambridge Journal VII:3 1953